Second Edition

BY
ANDRE RABE

ISBN: 978-0-9563346-6-4

Published by Andre Rabe Publishing.

Contents

Foreword   4

Introduction   8

Original and Authentic

1. Is this an Original?   12

2. An Intimate Picture   28

Shadows and Fragments

3. The Alternative   34

4. The Legal Picture   40

Substance and Completeness

5. Incarnation   52

6. Redemption   68

7. Word Pictures   82

End of all Dispute

8. The Contradiction of the Cross   92

9. Resurrection and victory   108

10. Ascension and new Reality   116

Conclusion

11. Confrontation   122

12. The Incarnation Continues   138

FOREWORD

If there ever was a time that the world needs to hear the truth of the Good News of Jesus Christ, it is now. Christ's appearing on the Earth was 2000 years ago, and little has changed in the condition of mankind since God sent His Son to us so that we should not perish. This is no indictment against God or the efficiency of His salvation, but rather it is evidence of the ignorance that has prevailed in our understanding of what the Gift of Christ really means to us.

Andre has taken the profound Good News of Jesus Christ and humanity's full inclusion in Him, and he has broken up the deep wells of truth so that the Water of Life gushes forth and washes over the mind, removing generations of religiosity that has clouded mankind's vision of Christ, and what remains is a clarity of understanding in the mind and heart of the reader that is astounding and breathtaking in it's brilliance.

"Imagine" takes you on an illuminating journey from God's original thought and intent before time began, right into man's conflicting experience within himself and with his God, and breaks through with the beautiful understanding of the Treasure that is in each one of us, redeemed and revealed in the Light that lights up every man - Christ.

Read it, digest it, be nourished with the Bread of Heaven;
and go awaken the sleeping with loud shouts of joy; tell
the World that Hope is here, and He lives in YOU.
...Colin Lagerwell

To imagine that God imagined me before time began
is the most liberating thought! It immediately gives
substance to faith and relevance to the gospel.
I matter to my Maker! He is mindful of me!
Andre's writing beautifully frames the picture that God
painted and exhibits it in the grand gallery of our own
reflections.
...Francois Du Toit

The revelation of the Logos, the Word of God, appeals to
more than our human intellect. It is the call of His Spirit
to our spirit. Jesus said: "the Words which I speak to you
are spirit and are life." (John 6:63) Natural words can
captivate your mind, but Spirit and Life go beyond your
mind and grasp your spirit man, your inner being. The
book Imagine… is such a call. The words contain more
than intellectual stimulation, they are 'spirit and life' for
your spirit and for your life.
...Jozsef Palavics M.D.

6

INTRODUCTION

IMPRESSIONISM

I loved art from an early age. I guess it's because my grandad was an artist. Although my grandparents stayed far away from us, we would always spend at least the summer holidays with them. It was an 8-10 hour road trip which, for a 5 year old boy, was the closest thing to 'eternity' I had ever experienced up to that age!

Vivid memories of the art studio still linger. The brushes and paints, the smells and atmosphere, the chaos of canvas sheets and half painted works of art, all these awakened such a sense of creativity. The beauty of the art works themselves stirred amazement at what is possible for a person to pull out of his imagination and place upon canvas for all to adore. How I wished I could join in the action, to grab a few of the brushes and become a co-artist with granddad. Unfortunately that was not allowed!

I definitely had my favourite paintings - the ones where the action of the artist was still evident, where the texture of a brush stroke or the flick of a palette knife was still clearly seen. In these pictures I not only saw the final polished image, but the thoughts of the artist, his boldness and freedom. The realisation that all these beautiful pictures came out of granddad's imagination, caused me to wonder what art lay hidden in me.

Art became my favourite subject at school. The one style that captured my imagination above all the others, is called Impressionism. This style of painting does not attempt to capture a photo-realistic image, but rather to simply give an impression, hence the name 'Impressionism'. The effects of light, movement and colour are combined in a way to capture the 'spirit' of an image rather than the facts. This has the effect of drawing the observer into an active participation, making a demand on one's imagination to complete the picture. Ironically, this style is able to portray more of the spirit and atmosphere of the actual scene than the styles that are obsessed with capturing each detail.

Jesus often taught using stories and conceptual pictures. I believe that God often speaks in this 'Impressionistic' way - a way that engages our imagination and makes a demand on our creative abilities to complete the picture.

In this book I want to paint some conceptual pictures in this Impressionistic style. The hope is that each reader will complete these pictures themselves - discover within your own imagination the ability to recognise truth and beauty.

Throughout the ages people have recognised the hand of an artist in creation.

David wrote:

The heavens declare the glory of God;
the skies proclaim the work of his hands.
Day after day they pour forth speech;
night after night they display knowledge. (Psalm 19)

But, nowhere is the boldness and creativity of this Artist better recognised than in the spirit of man. For in man's imagination, He has placed not only the ability to recognise beauty, but the ability to partake in the creative process of expressing the character of the greatest Artist - our Creator. He invites us to join in the action, to co-create with Him. All that is, began in His imagination. In seeing and adoring His artistry, the question is stirred, the possibility is awakened: what art lies hidden in me?

CHAPTER 1
IS THIS AN ORIGINAL?

... MORE THAN LANGUAGE ...

Mary-Anne and I were ministering in Budapest, Hungary once, when the eternal significance of this gospel became so pressing on me. Shortly before the service began, I became so aware that what we had to communicate was so much larger than my ability with language would allow, especially as everything I said would be translated into Hungarian.

Immediately I remembered that Paul experienced something very similar: "*You'll remember, friends, that when I first came to you to let you in on God's master stroke, I didn't try to impress you with polished speeches and the latest philosophy. I deliberately kept it plain and simple: first Jesus and who he is; then Jesus and what he did—Jesus crucified.*

I was unsure of how to go about this, and felt totally inadequate—I was scared to death, if you want the truth of it—and so nothing I said could have impressed you or anyone else. But the Message came through anyway. God's Spirit and God's power did it, which made it clear that your life of faith is a response to God's power, not to some fancy mental or emotional footwork by me or anyone else." (1 Cor 2:1-5 MSG)

Paul's feeling of inadequacy, or as some translations describe it, 'fear and trembling', was the result of seeing the enormity and significance of what he had to communicate and simultaneously realising the limitations of language and logic to do so. However, Paul discovered another truth: God is able to communicate Himself, to reveal Himself as He makes Himself the content of our declaration of the gospel.

As I stood before the few hundred people in Budapest, whose language I did not understand, I sensed the Lord saying: *Even if you were able to speak perfect Hungarian, you would still not be able to communicate the gospel! There is a supernatural element in the declaration of the gospel in which I (God) combine myself with the spirit of man and impart understanding that far exceeds human logic and the ability of the most eloquent language.* God reveals Himself. Our declaration simply establishes a connection through which He combines spirit with spirit.

With what peace and confidence I could speak, aware that God was doing what no language could ever do. God has no problem translating His exact thought into any language. In fact He is able to translate His mind into flesh! The ultimate destiny of God's Word - God's mind - has always been to become flesh. The most accurate and relevant translation is His expression through you! The scriptures point to a reality greater than themselves - they point to a substance in you! Christ in you is what it is all about.

... THE NATURE OF THIS WORD ...

The original, authentic Word was face to face with God from the very beginning. God Himself is the content of this communication - revealing His personal presence and unique expression in all that exists.

In fact there is nothing original or innovative outside of Him! He is the only Creator and the source of all inspiration and creativity. Everything that is, has 'Made by God' stamped on its existence.

The life that was in Him was made manifest in man - His life shines in man. (The very life of God is what ignited the existence of man) This original light still shines even in darkness and no amount of darkness can put this light out. (John 1:1-5 AR translation)

... ORIGINAL, AUTHENTIC AND PURE ...

The very first thing John has to say about this Word is that it is original and communicates the nearness of God. In fact, this word is inseparable from God. 'Original' means it is not derived, borrowed or the latest fad. This is what God intended from the start. Neither is this a message that has been passed on and adjusted through the course of time, but rather it is the pure, undiluted purpose of God. It is not subject to interpretation or mediation, this is the direct Word of God. If His own person is not the content of this gospel, then we are dealing with something other than the Word John spoke of. This Word is God!

Not only is this Word original, authentic and pure, but it reveals that you have your origin in Him. Consequently, you are an original! You are an authentic invention of the one and only Creator. The original motivation and creativity that gave you birth is revealed in this Word. Your identity, as God imagined it long before you were born, is displayed in all its purity and beauty by this Word. The 'additives' of time, the disappointments and achievements that veil your true substance is stripped away by this Word. Your true self, your uniquely-born-of-God self is revealed.

The most substantial, real existence you can have, is to exist in the mind of God. You were on his mind before the world began, and still you are the focus of His attention.

... NEAR AND INTIMATE WORD ...
It is understandable that a people who are alienated and confused about God would develop philosophies about His unknowability - or 'transcendence' for the theologically minded. And indeed this is true if we approach Him from our natural mind and reasoning. But in Christ He took

the initiative to make Himself known. This Word doesn't just communicate ideas about God. God communicates Himself in this Word. I'm so glad we don't have to occupy ourselves with our thoughts about God, because He has made His thoughts towards us, abundantly available. Become absorbed in His thoughts towards you.

No man has ever seen God at any time; the only unique Son of God, Who is in the bosom, in the intimate presence of the Father, He has declared Him [He has revealed Him and brought Him out where He can be seen; He has interpreted Him and He has made Him known]
(John 1:18 AMP)

There is no greater fulfilment than the intimate bosom of our Father, our Maker. Jesus, the unique Son of God has made that place of intimacy available. He reveals your own individuality and the Father's unique love for you. He is not ashamed to call you brother because we all have the same origin and in His Father's bosom is plenty of room. You too are a unique offspring of the Father from whom every family in heaven and earth derives its identity. (Eph 3:15)

... UNIQUE AND CREATIVE WORD ...

All of creation is testimony to the infinite creativity of our Creator. Despite the diversity we see in nature, it all points to the One Artist. When God thought of the ultimate expression of His creativity, the masterpiece of His artistic expression, the end result was mankind! This masterpiece would be a self-portrait: His vision of Himself, His likeness and image expressed with artistic skill upon the canvass of the human heart. However, each and every person would be a unique expression of His person. Unique ... but still a full expression of His person. In other words, we do not receive just a part of God, but 'of His fullness have we all received' - we receive all of God, yet we uniquely and individually represent Him.

Having been exposed to original works of art from an early age, I never developed a taste for copies or prints. No matter how vibrant the colours, the fact that a machine made duplicates of an original, the fact that the artist was not involved, seemed to rob such prints of so much of their spirit and beauty.

On a few rare occasions I was able to watch my granddad at work in his studio. The interaction of the artist and his work of art, the process and techniques can never be replaced by a mechanical counterfeit.

God is the Creator, not the duplicator! You are a unique artistic invention. The authentic thought of the one and only Creator found expression in you. The Artist was intimately involved in your creation.

... *Darkness did not overcome it* ...

The life that was in Him was made manifest in man - His life shines in man. (The very life of God is what ignited the existence of man) This original light still shines even in darkness and no amount of darkness can put this light out. John 1:4,5

The image and likeness that man was created in, is immutable - it cannot be destroyed. Darkness might have dimmed it, the father of lies might have obscured it, wickedness might have twisted man out of his true pattern, but the essence of man has never been completely destroyed.

Jesus came for no lesser purpose than to enlighten every man - to reveal our true origin and life-source. He did not come to a foreign race - He came to His own. This is why Paul had the confidence to say that we appeal to every man's conscience. (2 Cor 4:2)

... *The landscape of man's spirit* ...

There is a wisdom of a Godly kind
So pure and undefiled
It's the knowledge preserved within the heart
Of one who knew us and made us
From the very start...
(Extract from 'Original Design' - a song by Mary-Anne)

There is a wisdom that does not have its origin in this world, a wisdom that was not conceived by man. This wisdom began before creation, before time. It stands on its own, outside of time and space, yet is equally at home within this temporal realm. Although it manifests itself within creation, it is not confined to, or limited by creation. Time does not change it, no event can subtract from it. Yet it is relevant and specific to you. This wisdom has its reference in the heart and mind of God.

I recently watched a short documentary about the Augrabies National Park. One of the mightiest African rivers, the Molopo, once flowed through it, but the river hasn't flowed for more than a century. However, the evidence of the river is clearly seen. The landscape bears the 'memory' in the form of gorges and a broad river bed that have become a haven for all kinds of plants and animals. The reason the river hasn't flowed for so long is because the climate at the source has changed dramatically. There used to be heavy rainfalls at the source of the river, but they have ceased. However, should things change back, and should it once again be connected to a source of abundant water, the river will naturally flow again along the path that was carved hundreds, even thousands of years before.

The landscape of man's spirit, however dry and barren, still bears the memory of a once mighty river that flowed.

There remains a path, a ravine, in which the waters of the Word will flow naturally.

Our appeal is not limited to the natural intellect of man. In the same way as this wisdom does not originate in this world, so there is a part of man which has its origin in eternity. This eternal wisdom appeals to this eternal part of man. It is this common origin that causes a resonance, a recognition called 'faith', an innate response. "*All the ends of the world shall remember and turn to the LORD*" (Ps 22:27.) The Scriptures prophesy of an inherent, instinctive memory in all the world that will cause them to turn to the Lord.

And we are setting these truths forth in words not taught by human wisdom but taught by the [Holy] Spirit, combining and interpreting spiritual truths with spiritual language. (1 Cor 2:13 AMP) The literal translation simply says: "... *combining spirit with spirit*"

The content of this proclamation is more than concepts and ideas, it is the very Spirit of God that is communicated by these words. This type of conversation presents an opportunity for a fusion between man and God - this wisdom combines spirit with spirit. As naturally as a body of water flows into the gorges of a river, so these words flow and combine with the prepared channels within us.

For who has known or understood the mind (the counsels and purposes) of the Lord so as to guide and instruct Him and give Him knowledge? But we have the mind of Christ (the Messiah) and do hold the thoughts (feelings and purposes) of His heart. 1 Cor 2:14-16 AMP

What creature is there that has the capacity for this type of knowledge, this level of understanding? Who has the spiritual intelligence to have a meaningful conversation with God? Who can understand the mysteries hidden in Him? We can! God has unveiled His mind and all the mysteries in it, in Christ. He openly displayed His logic in such a way that we might accurately know Him. We now have a basis of meaningful conversation with Him. The mystery is no longer hidden; His thoughts are no longer concealed.

The natural order, worldly wisdom and human philosophy need not be our reference any longer. The Spirit of God has come and united Himself with us, so that we might know what He knows; so that we might see the significance of Christ as He sees it. He has come and given us the spiritual intelligence of Christ - '*We have the mind of Christ*'!

... *A TIMELESS PICTURE* ...

Imagine a dimension before time or space began. Imagine being present to hear the conversation within the God-counsel that planned and purposed all that is. What is it that motivated God to create?

Are you ready for a shocking truth? You were present! In fact you are the inspiration behind all of creation. God had you in mind even before the foundation of the earth and He is still just as excited about you as He was then!

The best place to begin is not the beginning but slightly before, so that we may understand why the beginning began. The original thought and motivation that gave birth to all of creation 'was' before time began. Speaking about this timeless realm means that we shouldn't really use time-related terms or tenses. A better way of saying the former would be: The original thought and motivation that gives birth and sustains all of creation, is before time began.

How do we understand timelessness? It's like asking an elephant to describe deep-sea diving - it's totally foreign to its natural environment! We exists within the context of time. Even our language is mostly bound to time. We use tenses to place our conversation in either the past, the present or the future. So how do we even approach a concept like timelessness?

Jesus completely messed up our tenses! He said things like: "*Before Abraham was, I am*". When we speak of the eternal realm, we speak about a realm very different from what we normally experience in this physical world. In time things decay. In eternity there is no decay. In time there is past, present and future. In timeless eternity there is no past or future as we observe it in our world, only something similar to what we call the present. Time began, Eternity is. Time is often defined as a sequence of events. As can be seen from 2 Tim 1:9, there definitely are events in eternity, however they are not bound to the past or the future. If there is a sequence, it is based on the significance of the event rather than 'time'.

But however alien this concept might sound, humans have always been intrigued by something strangely familiar about 'eternity'. Imagine walking into a cinema, half-way through the screening of a film. Having missed the beginning, it will probably take you a while to figure out the plot and understand the characters. Life is like a massive movie, that we joined halfway through the screening. We have all entered a story that began long before we were born. We are part of a very, very big story - it began before creation, but the director had you in mind even then! The scope of this plot is so vast that it makes the few years of our lives on earth seem insignificant, but they are not. You are an essential part of the director's plan; you are of irreplaceable value to Him.

Although we entered this story rather late, the Director wants to let us in on the whole story. The secret of understanding this plot from beginning to end is not out of reach - He preserved the script within you! "He has made everything beautiful in its time. Also, he has put eternity into man's heart, without which man cannot find out what God has done from the beginning to the end." (Eccl 3:11 LIT) God has placed eternity in our hearts so that we can have access into realms beyond the here and now, beyond the temporal, beyond the material.

... GRACE, BEFORE TIME BEGAN ...

The following scriptures speak of a realm before time began - a timeless dimension:

"God, who has saved us and called us with a holy calling, not according to our works, but according to His own purpose and grace, which was given to us in Christ Jesus before time began. This has now been made evident through the appearing of our Savior Christ Jesus, who has abolished death and has brought life and immortality to light through the gospel." (2 Tim 1:9)

"Long before he laid down earth's foundations, he had us in mind, had settled on us as the focus of his love, to be made whole and holy by his love. Long, long ago he decided to adopt us into his family through Jesus Christ. (What pleasure he

took in planning this!)" (Eph 1:4,5)

We are also assured that He did not leave the outcome to chance. He is not busy with an experiment and therefore He describes Himself as *"declaring the end from the beginning, and from ancient times the things that are not yet done, saying, My counsel shall stand, and I will do all my pleasure"* (Isa 46:10)

Romans 9 describes so beautifully the certainty of His purpose. It is not dependant on the good or bad that man does – He is not subject to our decisions. His purpose is solely dependant on His own decision and His own initiative:

... To Rebecca, also, a promise was made that took priority over genetics. When she became pregnant by our one-of-a-kind ancestor, Isaac, and her babies were still innocent in the womb–incapable of good or bad–she received a special assurance from God. What God did in this case made it perfectly plain that his purpose is not a hit-or-miss thing dependent on what we do or don't do, but a sure thing determined by his decision, flowing steadily from his initiative. (Rom 9:10-11 MSG)

There exists a timeless realm, a realm not subject to decay. What happens in this realm is immutable. What is declared in this realm, is unchangeable. What is given in this realm is irreversible. *"For God's gifts and His call are irrevocable."* - Rom 11:29

When John writes about the Word that was in the beginning (John 1:1), he refers to something much greater than a time-related event. The word he uses is 'ar-khay' which means chief (in various applications of order, time, place or rank): - beginning, first (estate), magistrate, power, principality, principle, rule.

So he speaks of that which is most important, most significant and most central. John is referring to the beginning of all beginnings, the origin of all origins, the first cause, the very essence of God's motivation.

Some might think that asking questions about, or peering into this mystery is futile because we are so far removed in time from that original event. But remember, we are speaking about a timeless event and therefore an event that is present! God's original motivation is as vibrant and real and urgent and inspiring right now as it has always been.

The life, death and resurrection of Jesus Christ happened within our time, but it was a manifestation of an eternal event. His appearance revealed what has always been true - the mystery hidden for ages and generations was finally made known in our dimension of time and space.

CHAPTER 2
AN INTIMATE PICTURE

... ORIGINAL MOTIVATION ...

Let's imagine this beginning, let's allow the spirit of God to draw us, just like He drew John, to this place in which all things had their origin. Although no science can explain it, although the greatest minds have tried and failed to define it, God is confident that you are able to comprehend the unsearchable; to appreciate the motivation that gave you birth; to remember where you began. In this place there is no space, yet no limit; no creation, yet no emptiness – there is only God in all His fullness.

This original motivation we speak of can be summarised in the word 'love'. But its not the mushy, confusing, temporal love that is often portrayed in movies or novels. This is a love that will make a demand on your understanding like nothing else you have ever encountered.

This is why Paul prayed in Eph 3:14-21 that you would be strengthened in your inner man, that you might be able to comprehend this love.

Have you ever seen a high-rise building while it is under construction? The amount of effort spent on foundations and structural reinforcement is amasing. Have you noticed the steel rods sticking out of the steel re-inforced concrete? All of this preparation is done for the sheer weight and volume of the building that will rely on this structure.

The sheer weight and volume of God's love, adoration and thoughts towards us need a reinforced container to receive them. We need to be strengthened by His spirit in the inner man to be able to comprehend. And so the revelation of this love cannot be separated from the person of God's spirit. It is He who is at work within us, preparing us, stretching us, strengthening us for the insight He brings.

He desires for us to explore the infinite boundaries of His love. Its limitless height; its unfathomable depth; its unreachable width; its unending length. And in discovering this love, find within ourselves the immeasurable capacity to contain it.

Let's explore a few of the dimensions of this love:

... *LOVE RECOGNISES VALUE* ...

This is no blind love - this is a love that recognises value, a love that sees more accurately, more deeply and more truly than any other. This love sees through every mask man has ever invented. Whether the mask is fashioned in the form of pride or shame makes no difference, for this love sees through any and every illusion.

I remember how amazed I was as a child to discover that God loved me in spite of all I had said and done, that was not worthy of love. My amazement has only grown as I have discovered that He not only loves me 'in-spite-of' but 'because-of'! In fact the reason that He loves us 'in-spite-of' is because He has a much greater reference than our words and deeds to base His love upon. The reason He can overlook so much is because He sees a reality of much greater significance. He looks deeper and recognises a value that is immutable.

Do the Scriptures not confirm that nothing is hidden before His eyes? (Heb 4:13) His love for us is based on what He sees - not on what He overlooks. And if His love is to be stirred in us, we need to see through His eyes.

What is it that He sees? What is it that He values? If I have to summarise it in one word, it would be the word 'likeness'.

... LOVE ADORES ...

Imagine two art critics looking at a painting such as 'Water Lilies' by Monet. Both might be aware that its market value is approximately £20 million, however, despite recognising this market value, one of them might not care for the painting much, while the other adores it. The one who adores it recognises a value beyond its price - its value is personal. This kind of appreciation creates a special bond between the one who adores and the object of adoration.

The beauty of the painting awakens appreciation in the observer and the way in which the observer looks at the painting unveils its beauty.

Our God adores us! Your value is very personal to Him. Your worth is so much larger than your market value. True value is only found in His adoration.

... LOVE'S REFLECTION ...

There is a sense in which one can love a pet. There is a sense in which one can love a specific location. But nowhere does love find fuller expression than in loving a being that is compatible with itself - a being of the same kind.

In Gen 2:18-25 we read one of the earliest stories of intimacy. Adam is in the process of naming all the animals and during this activity he becomes aware that there is no animal like himself. The Hebrew word neged refers to a counterpart or an opposite part, as in a mirror.

In verse 18 God says that it is not good for man to be alone. The word alone refers to a separate part. God's solution is to cancel this sense of separation and distance by introducing another part which is a mirror reflection of Adam; a counterpart; a distinct part but made to fit together.

Adam recognises Eve as bone of his bone and flesh of his flesh. He stands in awe at the woman who is distinct from him yet came out of him ... and their destiny is to be one. "*Adam and his wife were both naked, and they felt no shame.*" (verse 25) Such likeness is the basis for intimacy without shame and without hindrance. In referring to this very scripture, Paul wrote: "*This is a profound mystery—but I am talking about Christ and the church.*" (Eph 5:32)

Why is likeness such an important part of intimacy? Because love anticipates a response of equal quality! Love needs to be reflected for it to be fulfilled.

You were designed as the fulfillment of Love's dream. God joyfully anticipates a response of equal quality from you; His image and likeness reflected; His love returned. Love fully expects the real you, the true you to be made manifest.

... *LOVE MULTIPLIES* ...

When my second child was born, I did not have to halve the love I had for my first born in order to share it equally. Love multiplies. There is nothing selfish or insecure about love. In its very nature love is generous and gives liberally.

The individual intimacy God designed for us, is an intimacy so secure and full that it desires to include others.

Love is completed when it overflows beyond a two way exchange and embraces all that God designed for this embrace. It's a paradox - this intimacy remains individual and unique yet extends to include others in the same unique quality of love. This is the brilliance and the depth of the love of God.

CHAPTER 3
THE ALTERNATIVE

... NATURE AND ORIGIN OF EVIL ...

Many have asked the question: if God planned a perfect relationship, then why was there an alternative and why did the alternative last so long? Why the fall of humanity in Adam, and why the thousands of years before salvation came in Christ?

It is precisely because there is only one quality of relationship that can satisfy, that the alternative had to be given every opportunity to succeed. For in giving the alternative all the necessary time and every possible opportunity to succeed, its failure and destruction would be final and beyond dispute.

When God considered all the possibilities and all the options in creating the environment in which His love dream for man would be fulfilled, there were many possibilities that He rejected. Evil is all the possibilities that God rejected. Evil is everything God chose not to create. Evil is not eternal; it is not to be compared with God or even God's creation in any way. Evil does not have an eternal past nor an eternal future - it is doomed to pass away.

So, if God did not create evil, how did it come into being?

It is useful to look at the symbolism used in the scriptures to describe evil.

Darkness is used to describe evil, ignorance, lies, and all that has no substance in itself, no eternal significance.

Light is used to describe God Himself, understanding, truth and that which has substance; that which has eternal significance.

Darkness has no substance in itself - it is the absence of light. It only 'exists' in the absence of substance, which is not a real existence at all. It only has a form of existence in its opposition to that which truly exists. It's only content is nothingness. God never created darkness - He created light. Darkness is the un-created opposition to that which God chose to create.

Before God created, there was no evil. In a sense, evil is the potential by-product of creation - it is everything that God did not create.

Everything that is good: love, joy, peace, have their basis within a person ... the person of God. Evil, however, does not have its origin in a person, but in that which is impersonal, that which apposes the person of God and all He has made. Obviously, evil can find expression through a personality if it is given opportunity to do so. If a human gives space to evil, inhumanity is the result. Evil is not a natural attribute of humanity - it is inhuman to its core.

All of this might sound very theoretical and abstract, but evil found a very real and concrete opportunity to express itself in our world. But how can it, if it has no real existence, if its very nature is unreal and uncreated?

... MAN'S PART IN GIVING EVIL AN OPPORTUNITY ...

When God planned the end even before the beginning, He knew that man, created in His own image and likeness, would have the creative abilities and the power to choose the possibilities that He rejected. However, there was no other way in which to create the ultimate companion, except by giving man this creative freedom.

Man would be capable of choosing the possibilities that He rejected, choosing to give time and space to that for which God has no time nor space; that which He did not create. Man, represented by Adam and Eve, did exactly that. They chose to believe a lie, to embrace what was unreal, uncreated, and in so doing became untrue. They let go of their true existence in God and instead clung to the nothingness of separation.

This alternative is called the kingdom of darkness. It

represents an unreal existence; self-importance without substance; living in ignorance, death and separation; accepting an identity not created by God, an identity that is not authentic nor original. The ultimate goal of this kingdom is to reduce man to the same nothingness from which it came.

In the real existence of man, evil found opportunity to express its opposition to everything that God made. Man, as the ruler of creation and the ultimate companion of God, gave darkness - the uncreated and unreal, the absence of light - a very real opportunity to manifest its opposition to everything that is good and created by God. Adam's fall gave evil a very tangible existence in this new world of illusions and deception. All of creation was subjected to corruption as it was drawn towards nothingness.

Adam and Eve were given stewardship over all creation. Their actions would affect all of creation. When they gave evil space in the created world, all of creation became subject to corruption, drawn towards the non-existent nothingness that is evil. Man himself was drawn towards this opposition to all that is God and of God, meaning that man even opposed himself, resisted himself and denied his true existence in God.

Man embraced illusions as his reality, instead of allowing

reality itself to embrace him. The possibility of self-importance tempted man into an existence without substance. Living in death and separation was preferred above discovering the secret of life in our union with Christ in God. Instead of living out of the reality of I AM, man succumbed to the suggestion of 'I am not'.

... *TREE OF KNOWLEDGE OF GOOD AND EVIL* ...

The knowledge of good and evil is the alternative to simply and spontaneously living from the source of all life. We were designed to reflect Him, to behold His adoration and mirror it back. When we ost sight of God, we began looking at one another and reflecting our own confusion. This moral awareness offers an alternative to direct and intimate relationship with God. It promises an independent way of living a good life. God was clear about the consequence of eating from this tree: "you must not eat from the tree of the knowledge of good and evil, for when you eat from it you will certainly die". This death is not ceasing to exist, it is separation from the source of life.

This alternative only seemed attractive because man never fully grasped the intimacy, the knowledge of oneness, that was available in God. Ignorance makes sin attractive. So the core problem was not the deed of sin nor the act of disobedience. These were simply the symptoms of the core problem which was: man did not know the Father in the intimate way in which He wanted to be known. Later we'll see that Jesus' mission was not only to deal with deeds of sin and the guilt of sin, but to solve the core problem, namely: to make the Father known. For in doing that, sin loses all its attraction.

CHAPTER 4
THE LEGAL PICTURE.

Marriage is meant for intimacy and enjoyment - suspicion and distance undermine the very purpose of marriage. One can never replace the spontaneity and freedom of being in love, with formality and obligation and still maintain the same quality of relationship.

Lets imagine a scenario in which a husband and wife have had a fight, and seeing that it's just a fantasy, lets say it's all the wife's fault! The husband tries to converse, but the situation is so tender that the wife can't face any further confrontation. Silence and distance become her only escape.

Through the days and weeks that follow the situation only gets worse and this results in a separation. The husband observes his wife sinking into a pit of depression but she is not willing to face him or converse with him. However the husband still loves his wife and believes that the relationship can be restored, so he makes a practical interim arrangement. In order to prevent her from falling into absolute destitution and despair, he commits to support her and provide for her if she keeps to some basic and reasonable obligations. For instance: remain faithful to him - no other lovers allowed! Very reasonable. A few other 'boundaries' are agreed - about 10 in all. All this is done for her protection.

The only thing these arrangements are supposed to reveal, is that the husband still believes that the relationship can be saved. These arrangements were never meant to replace the original intimate relationship. They were only put in place for her protection and provision until the original relationship is restored. By no means can this situation compete or compare with the spontaneous, intimate relationship they once enjoyed.

Something terrible happens in this arrangement: It gives validity to the distance! The very distance that needs to be destroyed, finds an opportunity within this temporary arrangement to make itself legitimate. This new law-system gives validity to the distance!

The wife, instead of trying to find a fundamental solution to the problem, now hides behind the fact that she is keeping the rules and therefore deserves the provision. She actually finds this new system very convenient, because she does not have to deal with her husband directly. She feels justified in keeping the rules, and even when she breaks the rules there are ways of correcting the situation without direct contact with him. Her heart grows even harder!

... THE LAW IS TEMPORAL ...

The law was never meant to solve the relationship between man and God - it was only an interim arrangement. In a way it revealed something of the heart of God - He still believed the relationship could be restored. But the law was not the way in which He would restore the relationship - it was only given in the context of mankind falling into total destitution and chaos, as an interim way of protecting and providing for man. In Christ the Law is both fulfilled and removed, as He restored the intimacy and freedom of the original relationship.

... THE LAW DOES NOT SOLVE THE PROBLEM ...

The law never dealt with sin, never brought sin to a final judgement. In fact the problem was intensified within this context. Sin - which was the very distance and separation that resulted from this broken relationship - found an opportunity within the law system. Distance gained a form of validity in the Law! And man, instead of gratefully accepting the provision, uses the law to develop self-righteousness. The Law served to harden man's heart even further. Man used the Law to offer an outward obedience, without any inner transformation.

... SIN IS STRENGTHENED BY THE LAW ...

Only in the context of a humanity that was separated from God, a humanity without intimate relationship with God, was the Law given. The Law, given by God for man's protection, is good in itself. However, it created an environment in which sin strengthened itself by the seemingly legitimate distance that the Law maintained. Paul said it this way: "But sin, that it might appear sin, was producing death in me through what is good, so that sin through the commandment might become exceedingly sinful" (Rom 7:13) Sin's voice of condemnation is strengthened by the very Law of God that confirms the inadequacy of man to consistently live up to God's standards.

... BONDAGE OF THE LAW ...

The difference, the distance between that which 'is' and that which 'ought to be' is emphasized by the law. This constant strain between what you are and what you ought to be, results in an increased sense of distance. Man feels self-righteous when keeping the Law, and condemned when breaking it and neither situation brings man any closer to the intimacy He desires! It's a lose-lose situation: whether man keeps the law or breaks it, he will be no closer to God! And so the very Law, given by God, good in itself, becomes a bondage.

... BONDAGE OF RELIGION & LAW TOGETHER ...

For people who are not interested in intimate relationship with God, the law system is very convenient, for they do not have to deal with God directly. Even when the laws are transgressed, there is a whole system of sacrifice and ritual in place to restore this law-relationship without ever meeting God face to face. The law became the veil, the separation, that kept man from direct contact with God. The religious rituals and the law worked together to maintain a level of relationship, but never restored the original relationship and in so doing, religion became a bondage as well.

... GOD'S STRATEGY WITH THE LAW ...

God did not make a mistake when He gave the Law, neither was He unaware that the Law would in itself not solve the problem of separation. He knew and purposely designed the Law in such a way that it would intensify the conflict - that it would reveal the problem for what it really was and reveal man's impotence to solve the problem by himself. He designed this environment of conflict - a conflict that was working its way towards a climax. "*Therefore the law is holy, and the commandment holy and just and good.*" (Rom 7:12). In its context, it served the purpose of God. Outside of this context it becomes a man-made evil system of oppression.

Under the Law, man and God never met face to face. Instead of direct contact with God, the Law became the intermediary by which man related to God based on a knowledge of good and evil, right and wrong. The Law maintained the distance between God and man and in so doing, prolonged and intensified the conflict.

Although the law was not designed to solve the problem of separation, it was designed to reveal the problem. The Law revealed another law or government. Paul says that under the Law, he discovered another law or government at work within him. "*For I delight in the law of God according to the inward man. But I see another law in my members, warring against the law of my mind, and bringing me into captivity to the law of sin which is in my members.*" (Rom 7:21,22) The experience of man under the law, was that there was a stronger influence in man that forced him to live contrary to what he knew was right. The flesh became the domain of sin and man by himself was helpless to change the situation. And so Paul continues in verse 23: "*O wretched man that I am! Who will deliver me from this body of death? I thank God—through Jesus Christ our Lord!*"

The fullness of time was drawing near in which the final judgement upon sin and self-righteousness would be complete. "*But when the fullness of the time had come, God sent forth His Son, born of a woman, born under the law, to redeem those who were under the law, that we might receive the adoption as sons.*" Gal 4:4,5

God was preparing to enter the domain of sin - flesh. He

was preparing to enter the strong man's house, bind him and spoil his goods. *"For what the law was powerless to do because it was weakened by the flesh, God did by sending his own Son in the likeness of sinful flesh to be a sin offering. And so he condemned sin in the flesh,"* (Rom 8:3) He came to take back every part of humanity that He created, including flesh!

... *MODERN RELIGIOUS LAW SYSTEM* ...

So many scriptures make it clear that in Christ Jesus, God has invalidated the Law system. In Christ Jesus, God meets with us face to face. Consequently we read *"But now the righteousness of God apart from the law is revealed"* (Rom 3:21) Every barrier, including the law, that stood between man and God was removed in Christ. Nothing but the original, intimate, face to face relationship He had in mind, will satisfy.

But now we have been delivered from the law, having died to what we were held by, so that we should serve in the newness of the Spirit and not in the oldness of the letter. Rom 7:6

In Christ Jesus we have also been freed from the control of sin and death! "For the law of the Spirit of life in Christ Jesus has made me free from the law of sin and death.* Rom 8:2

However, man-made religion depends on the law-system

to maintain control and give itself a form of validity. Many teachings and systems that label themselves as Christian, have simply changed their terminology to sound more like the New Testament, but in reality they perpetuate the old, and now invalid, law-system.

I call this the new law-system, because this is an attempt to re-make the old law-system into something that is valid for today. In this 'new' law-system, the commandments and rules become principles. Instead of actual animal sacrifices, they promote personal sacrifices of time and especially money as a way to guarantee God's favour. Even the gifts of God are reduced to benefits that can be earned through diligently following the precepts laid out by the new professional priesthood.

Instead of a consciousness of union, there is a constant awareness of right and wrong. There is a constant awareness of man's contribution: Have I followed the seven steps to ensure that I'm in the will of God; have I applied the three steps to receiving from God correctly?! To declare with Paul that *"it is no longer I that live but Christ who lives in me, and the life I now live, I live by the faith of the son of God"*, seems like a mystical paradox.

This new law-system is present in some of the most current and modern religious movements, yet the bondage and separation that results from it is as old as sin itself. Anything that denies man the intimate, immediate and unconditional encounter with God, denies the reality of what Christ achieved, no matter how spiritual it sounds!

... NOTHING TO ADD ...

Anything that promotes any sense of distance between man and God, is as invalid as the law.

This is final: I have deleted the record of your sins and misdeeds. I no longer recall them. (Nothing in God's reference of man, reminds him of sin.) Sins were dealt with in such a thorough manner that no further offerings would ever again be required. Nothing that we can personally sacrifice could add further virtue to our innocence. Brethren, this means that, through what the blood of Jesus communicates and represents, we are now welcome to access this ultimate place of sacred encounter with unashamed confidence. (Hebrews 10:17-19 Mirror Translation)

The whole basis of our relationship with God is that Christ removed all distance - he who is joined to the Lord is one spirit with Him. The revelation of Christ in me and His perfect workmanship in man, leaves me without any consciousness of my contribution, only with an overwhelming consciousness of gratitude.

Let's imagine I was the steward of a great art collection, including a very rare Picasso painting. One day I decide that in my opinion, Picasso missed a brush stroke and made the colour of a flower too bright. I therefore get some paint and a brush to correct the Masterpiece! My contribution will not add to the value of the painting, in fact it will subtract from its value! Christ's masterpiece of redemption should simply be adored and enjoyed. If we think our contribution can add anything to it, we are delusional.

... *The Perfect Law of Liberty* ...

The new covenant knows of only one valid law - the law of life in Christ Jesus. This has nothing to do with your effort, self discipline or contribution, but everything to do with discovering yourself, your life, in Christ Jesus.

James calls it the perfect law of liberty. The law of liberty sounds so contradictory. Laws are designed to limit freedom, to restrict movement, to control. But the law of liberty is very different. In verse 1:23 James says that if any man hears this Word he is like a man that sees the face of his birth as in a mirror. Then James continues by saying that the secret of living according to our original design is looking deeply into the perfect law of liberty ... and continuing therein. This law demands that once you see yourself you do whatever you please! God knows that your true self has nothing in itself that is offensive to Him.

The law of life in Christ Jesus, the perfect law of liberty simply states: Know yourself and be yourself. The secret of your life is your union with Christ in God. In Christ Jesus, God and man meet, what 'is' and what 'ought to be' is united and in so doing every difference, every gap, every possible sense of separation is destroyed.

Chapter 5
The Incarnation

... What no one could imagine ...

Throughout the ages God revealed fragments of His mind. The Old Testament is a record of the many prophets, priests and scholars, scattered throughout many generations, who perceived portions of God's purpose. The best scholars steeped themselves into detailed studies, trying to piece together this puzzle. The priests diligently performed their rituals, aware that the very repetition of these rituals pointed towards an event and meaning that would eclipse their activities.

A picture started to emerge ... and it was shocking. All the fragments joined together, all the prophetic utterances stitched together painted a picture of ... a shadow! However amazing these revelations were, they were still only a shadow of what God was about to unleash. The substance behind the shadow was about to appear!

Despite the thousands of years of inspired utterance and scholastic studies, there remained a mystery which no eye had seen, no ear had heard - a mystery beyond the capability of any imagination!

No one except God could ever have conceived such a plan: Eternity would enter time; the infinite would enter space. God would become a man!

The Word, the expression of God, the exact representation of God became flesh! This was no half-hearted attempt by which God simply disguised Himself in a human body. This was a permanent commitment by which God forever joined Himself to humanity - His eternal destiny bound up in the destiny of man. He became man in the fullest sense possible and would remain a man forever.

The authentic Creator, the true light that enlightens every man was coming into this world. His mission was nothing less than shattering our illusions, exposing the unreal, unoriginal and fake identity that we embraced outside of Him. He came with the clear message to darkness that its time was up. Darkness has had all the opportunity it needed and failed to fulfill man, failed to provide a viable alternative. The incarnation reveals that our true selves, our true humanity can only be found in union with God.

Jesus brings the final and thorough judgement that the law failed to bring: judgement on the ignorance and lies that man so desperately embraced. The emptiness and futility of separation is exposed by Christ.

Simultaneously He introduces us to our true substance, to our existence in Him. The Creator became part of creation to redeem it from the grasp of corruption. In the incarnation He draws His creation back into the significance and value for which He created it. He reveals our true significance, our eternal origin and destiny in Him.

... *FULLY GOD* ...

Jesus represents God in the fullest, truest sense possible. Jesus not only represents God, He is God. What He says, God says; what He does, God does. Jesus Himself said "if you've seen me, you've seen the Father". Paul wrote in 2 Cor 5:19 that God was in Christ reconciling the world to Himself.

The implications of this incarnation are staggering! God became man without ceasing to be God. Jesus boldly declares "... *before Abraham was, I AM.*" Neither did this transformation, this form of existence as a man, frustrate God. In fact Col 1:19 shows that this was a pleasure! Col 2:9 reveals that God in all His fullness found expression in the body of Christ Jesus! Man is God-compatible!

God does not consider the human body an embarrassment to His desire to reveal and express Himself. He knows that our very existence is the result of His artistic expression to portray His image and likeness. The most accurate and exact reflection of God was revealed in the man Jesus Christ. "...*Jesus is the radiant and flawless expression of the person of God. He makes the glory (intent) of God visible and exemplifies the character and every attribute of God in human form.*" (Heb 1:3) Christ did not come to bring another dim or obscure view, but a full and complete and crystal clear view of our Father and our likeness to Him.

Whatever the Word was in God, before the incarnation, He now is within human form. He was not reduced in person or expressive ability when He became man. He is still the eternal Word, present to God, face to face with God, the mirror image of God, who Himself is God ... and is man. To exist as a man was His plan from the beginning.

So in the person of Christ God gave unhindered expression to Himself and in so doing, revealed what He was really like. Jesus is the revelation of the true identity and character of God. Against a backdrop of rituals and laws and judgements which confused so many about the character of God, He shows up personally to remove every misconception. He is not vengeful - He is willing to suffer the consequences of our sin for us. He is not easily offended, but rather at the peak of our enmity against Him, He is willing to reconcile us to Himself even while we were still dead in our trespasses and sins.

God is often described in lofty terms such as: Omnipresent (present everywhere); Omniscient (all knowing); Omnipotent (all powerful). However, in becoming man in Christ Jesus, He limits Himself to a single location; we read that He grew in knowledge and wisdom, and that in His home town He could not do many mighty works because of their unbelief. Despite the fact that Jesus was no longer omnipresent, omniscient or omnipotent, God was still able to fully be Himself in Christ! Why? Because in essence God is love and the human existence is not in any way an inferior expression of His love or life.

He lived fully and continues to express Himself without constraint in the man Christ Jesus! Our humanity is not a constraint to God's ability to fully and freely express Himself. You are not a frustration to God, you are His opportunity to be.

Jesus did not come to change the heart and mind of God concerning man, but to chance our minds about God. He came to reveal the truth about God and about us and in so doing make us true - genuinely ourselves.

"God, who has saved us and called us to a holy life—not because of anything we have done but because of his own purpose and grace. This grace was given us in Christ Jesus before the beginning of time, but it has now been revealed

through the appearing of our Savior, Christ Jesus, who has destroyed death and has brought life and immortality to light through the gospel." 2 Tim 1:9,10

God's mind and attitude towards us was established before time began. He gave us grace - gave us Himself even before we were born, before we could do anything to deserve it, or not deserve it. Before we had any opportunity to impress or disappoint Him, He was already impressed - impressed with the image and likeness He stamped upon our beings. From His point of view we were found before we were lost - He found us in Christ long before we were lost in Adam. We were given grace before the fall. He was simply waiting for the opportune time in which to appear - in which to reveal what has always been: the reality of our salvation in Christ Jesus.

... FULLY MAN ...

God became man in the fullest sense possible - He embraced humanity in this act of incarnation to such an extent that all of humanity would be represented in His person. The extent to which He became man, is the extent to which this salvation is reality to us. We were in His life, His death, His resurrection and His ascension. He took humanity upon Himself, within Himself, with such intensity that God would consider His every act as the act of man. His accomplishments would be credited to the account of mankind. He represents man more completely, truly and fully than any other man.

Your birth did not take God by surprise! When you showed up on planet earth, is not when He found out about you. He knew you before you were born. He was intimately acquainted with your design and chose you individually before time began.

What He knew about you before your birth is still His only reference for who you are. Your successes or failures have not changed His mind about you. Love never stops believing the best; never stops hoping; never runs out of patience and love never fails.

He knows the truth about you. Eph 1:13 describes this message as the "*word of truth - the gospel of your salvation*" This is the good news of the reality of what God did for you and of what Jesus did on your behalf: He redeemed your original design.

We often read, especially in theological books, about the nature of man. (It's interesting that this term is rarely used in the scriptures.) So I did some research as to what most theologians mean by 'nature of man'. It means the truth or reality of man!

That is such a clear and simple definition - the problem is that many try to find the truth and reality of man in Adam's fall. We should look a bit further back and discover Gen 1:26 - The truth and reality of man came out of God. His nature was the origin of our nature. His reality is the substance we were made from!

The key to understanding the mystery of God-and-man-in-the-one-person-of-Christ, is to realise that He designed man for this very purpose of unity with God. There is no conflict in God's design between the nature of man and the nature of God.

Man is God's idea. And so when God became man it was the original, authentic idea of man that manifested in the person of Christ - the perfect man. What God always knew to be true of man suddenly burst upon the stage of human history. "*The true light that gives light to every man was coming into the world.*" John 1:9 He is the light that reveals the truth about all of humanity, and to each one individually. The revelation He brings is "...full of grace and truth".

The fact that God was able to become man, is testament to the integrity of our design. When He originally created man saying: "*Be our image and our likeness*", He did not create an inferior creature to Himself - He created exactly what he said: His own mirror reflection in form and substance. In Jesus we recognise God as bone of our bone and flesh of our flesh. This likeness is the basis for intimacy without shame and without hindrance.

... PLAN A ...

The story of Adam and Eve has sometimes been presented as God's first attempts at relationship with man. However the fall forced Him to think of an alternative. That is not true.

The need for the incarnation did not surprise God - He planned this before the fall. The incarnation - the event in which God would become man - was His idea from the start. The fall did not necessitate redemption; redemption was planned before the fall.

He did not simply endure being human for 33 years and then, with great relief, returned to being God! 1 Tim 2:5, was written after the resurrection and ascension and reveals that Christ Jesus is still a man: "*For there is one God and one Mediator between God and men, the Man Christ Jesus*". The incarnation is permanent. He united Himself with Humanity in such a way that He would never be separated again. He bound Himself to our existence; committed Himself to our destiny. The resurrection is proof that this God-man union is not a temporary event, but an eternal unbreakable union.

God has invested everything He has, everything He is, in mankind. He has no other investment, no other interest, no other occupation than you! He believes in you, He is fully committed to you. "...*How many are Your thoughts toward me, how vast the sum of them...*" Ps 139:17

... *ALL OF MANKIND* ...

Authentic speaks of that which is original. The truth about man, the authentic truth about you, is found in your origin. There is a greater reference and definition of man, than Adam's fall. God individually knew us even before the fall of this world. The opposite of authentic, is derived or fake. Adam chose an unoriginal, unauthorised and fake identity, but the original reality from which man came remained preserved in Christ.

As surely as all mankind was represented in Adam and effected by His act of disobedience, so the same mass of humanity was included in the undeserved gift of Christ. (Rom 5:12-21) Christ is called the last Adam - this not only points to His uniqueness but to the fact that He brought a final end to the old Adamic race, a race identified by sin and the consequent guilt and judgement. In His death all and each one of that race died and in His resurrection, mankind - everyone of us - was restored to blameless innocence before God.

He is not only the last Adam, but He is God's original thought of man - the original man. Eph 4 refers to Him as the perfect man. He came to unveil God's authentic thought about man, to restore man to the image and likeness for which He designed us; to break the dormancy of the DNA of God that remained hidden, in lifeless seed form, in each man; to remind mankind that we belong, that we have the image of our owner stamped upon our being.

In Christ, God took decisive action to restore and bring you back to what He always had in mind. Christ reveals that God has made a decision concerning you, and that decision is to unite you with Himself. God is not slowly making up His mind about mankind as a whole or you individually as He observes your choices and actions. No! He made up His mind before He created you and determined that you would stand blameless before Him, enveloped in His love. Christ Jesus makes known what God decided about you: He believes in you!

... *PERSONAL* ...

This is no impersonal generic philosophy - this Word is as personal as a mirror. In a mirror, you see yourself. James wrote that if any man hears this word, he sees the face of his birth (origin) as in a mirror. When God became man,

He did not only embrace humanity, He embraced you personally. He wants you to discover yourself in Him.

There is a vast difference between a shop window and a mirror. A shop window simply reveals potential - what you could have, could buy, could attain. A mirror reveals reality - what is. Jesus is so much more than a moral example for us to follow, so much more than a shop window that shows us what could be possible. He reveals the present reality of our identity.

"And all of us, as with unveiled face, [because we] continued to behold [in the Word of God] as in a mirror the glory of the Lord, are constantly being transfigured into His very own image..." 2 Cor 3:18 Amp

Jesus is the mirror that unveils our true face. He reveals that God did not make a mistake when He declared you to be His very own image. Beholding this reality transforms every aspect of our lives.

You were represented in Him. He embraced your humanity. His death was your death; His judgement was your judgement; His resurrection was your resurrection; His glorification is yours; His blameless innocence is yours. His faith is a gift to you so that you no longer have to live by your own convictions, but by the faith of the son of God -

live from His point of view! His life is now your life - you no longer have to live yourself, live Him! (Gal 2:20, 2 Cor 5:15)

The incarnation continues: you are God's opportunity to continue to live and move and have His being amongst His own; His opportunity for the gift of truth and grace to continue in visible form; His opportunity for the light of life to continue to shine, for the revelation of the Father to continue to surprise humanity with His goodness. In you He has a face. In you He has a personality. Christ continues and you are His body.

... GOD AND MAN UNITED ...

Jesus is the union of God and man without separation, division or confusion. He fully represents God, in fact He is God. He fully represents man, in fact He is a man. The following is a short summary of what this union means:

Jesus is God's initiative to reconcile and embrace humanity and He is man's perfect response to that initiative. He is both God's judgement and man's perfect acceptance of that judgement. He is both God's act of salvation and man's response of perfect faith.

When God became man in Christ, He became the man that God always had in mind. As such He does not represent just one single man, but all of humanity.

In Christ God dealt with the old Adamic race, having forgiven all their sin. In Christ, humanity shed its old sinful identity and received the blameless innocence provided by God. In Christ, God raised humanity to a new level of existence - seated at His right hand. In Christ, humanity responded by taking up this new position to reign and rule in life.

His death was the death of the fallen Adamic race. His resurrection was the birth of a new victorious humanity. His resurrection demonstrates that this union of God and man was not a temporary arrangement, but an eternal reality - God embraced humanity in Christ never to be separated again. This God-man union faced hell and death and came through in-tact.

His ascension is the restoration of man to the place and position that God always intended for man to occupy. If the incarnation was an act in which God humbled Himself to take on human form, then the ascension is an act of glorification in which man is restored to a place of honour and completeness.

Jesus Christ is simultaneously God's invitation, and man's acceptance; He is God's call and man's answer; He is God's revelation and man's response of faith.

So what is left to do? Wake up! Shake off the slumber of what seems to be real around you and see your true self - your embraced-by-God-self.

Awake to the reality of your true identity:

As for me, I will behold thy face in righteousness: I shall be satisfied, when I awake in thy likeness. Ps 17:15

Awake to the reality of your new position:
Pursue with diligence the consequence of your co-inclusion in Christ. Relocate yourself mentally! His resurrection co-raised you to the same position of authority, seated in the strength of God's right hand. Becoming affectionately acquainted with Throne Room thoughts will keep you from being distracted again by the earthly (soul-ruled) realm. Your union with His death broke the association with that world; the secret of your life now is the fact that you are wrapped up with Christ in God. Col 3:1-3 Mirror Translation

Awake, awake - the nightmares and contradictions are part of a temporary slumber. There are eternal realities to be discovered! Awake!

The practical implications of this God-man union in Christ

are overwhelming! It means that my relationship with God is not based on my obedience, but on the obedience of this one man. It means that even my 'faith' is not mine – the faith I present to the Father has its origin in Christ and its perfection in Christ (He is the Author and perfecter of my faith)

CHAPTER 6
REDEMPTION

... ENTER THE MIND OF CHRIST ...

What does the life, death and resurrection of Jesus Christ have to do with me? It's an event that happened thousands of years before I was born - how can it have any relevance to my life? There is no theoretical or logical way to explain this connection. That is why Paul said that to the Greeks, who sought to know God through human wisdom, this message is pure foolishness.

For us to grasp this connection, to understand our own personal inclusion in Christ, we have to go beyond theory - we need to enter the reality and the mind of God. Our union with Him cannot even be unveiled through miraculous signs and wonders! There is a realm of understanding far deeper than spectacular signs, far wiser than human logic. Let's allow the Spirit of God to draw us into the mind of Christ right now.

The event of Christ - His story - is of such significance that it has a greater relevance and claim upon your existence than your own personal history! The event of Christ, although manifest in human history, is an eternal event and therefore not bound to the temporal. Yes it most definitely happened within our human history, but it is different from all other human history in that it did not pass away with time - it is as real and present today as it has always been.

It is in this context that I want us to explore the life of Christ. His life is so much more than historic fact, it is the revelation of your true life.

History records the facts of Jesus' life, eternity records the truth of its meaning. In the event of Christ, fact and truth meet as the Eternal One enters our time; time and eternity coincide. God's reality entered our time and became concrete fact within our human history. However, this historic fact still communicates timeless truth and remains a manifestation or appearance of what has always been and still is true.

... THE WORD BECAME FLESH ...

Reconciliation is not an act that was limited to the death and resurrection of Christ - reconciliation began in the incarnation. The incarnation was the act in which God and man were brought together in harmony. The person of Christ cannot be separated from the work of reconciliation. Salvation is in Him, redemption is in Him. He has been made our wisdom, our righteousness, our holiness and our redemption. (1 Cor1:30)

Mediator normally refers to a third party who stands between two other parties - in the gap - in order to make peace or negotiate a deal. However, Christ is a completely different type of mediator: God and man come face to face in this one person, Christ Jesus. He is not a third party; He is God and He is man. This is the perfect mediation in which man faces God directly and God faces man directly and brings about a perfect harmony in the person of Christ.

The Word became flesh. (John 1:14) John chooses the word flesh. He could have said the word became man, but he chooses the word *flesh*. Why? Of all the attributes of man, our intellect, our social interaction, our spirituality, flesh is the most base. Flesh represented the arena of conflict, the environment in which temptation thrived. Flesh became the domain of sin. Jesus becomes man in every respect because only that which He becomes, does He save.

Jesus did not arrive on this earth with supernatural protection against the evil that plagues humanity. It was into this domain of conflict, into our humanity with all its contradictions, temptation and weakness that Christ entered. The reign of death, the bondage and the curse introduced by Adam and the consequent righteous judgement of God, was the human condition into which Christ was born. And so Paul writes: "*But when the fullness of the time had come, God sent forth His Son, born of a*

woman, born under the law, to redeem those who were under
the law, that we might receive the adoption as sons." (Gal.
4:4,5 NKJV)

The true light entered the kingdom of darkness and refused
to be dimmed or put out. The true man entered fallen
humanity but refused to submit to the lie of a lesser identity.
He knew that sin was not an attribute of true humanity,
but an attribute of inhumanity. He entered a humanity
at enmity against God, but refused to allow His view and
knowledge of God to be perverted, refused to see God as
the enemy. He brings the conflict to a climax and in so
doing, He condemns sin in the flesh. *"For what the law*
could not do in that it was weak through the flesh, God did by
sending His own Son in the likeness of sinful flesh, on account
of sin: He condemned sin in the flesh" Rom 8:3 NKJV

He fully identified with fallen man, fully subjected himself
to the battles with which sinful man struggled ... yet He
remained sinless. The baptism of John was a baptism of
repentance - that is why John objected to Christ being
baptised. But the baptism of repentance was part of Christ
representing man, identifying Himself with sinful man and
repenting on their behalf. This was part of Christ fulfilling
all righteousness - meeting the righteous demands made
upon man under the law.

It is in the very act of becoming flesh that the redemption of the flesh begins, that the dominance of sin was broken and man was restored to liberty and freedom from a foreign ruler. He becomes the last Adam; He brings to an end the dominion of sin and death in man. By His perfect obedience within this flesh, He exposes the lie of the kingdom of darkness and brings to a final end the race of humanity that lived in subjection to this false identity. In so doing He becomes the firstborn of the new creation. The first man in whom God is not frustrated or limited by flesh, but in Christ the fullness of the Godhead dwells in bodily form.

Christ is the last Adam. There is such a finality about the effect of Christ's obedience. To be part of, or identified by, the disobedience of Adam is no longer an option. Sin no longer defines man! Christ unveiled our true identity! I've unfortunately heard so many messages that portray the effect of Adam's fall as equally relevant and valid as the effect of Christ's obedience. There is no comparison! Christ undid what Adam did; He found what Adam lost; He brought liberty and life to humanity. How long are we going to allow such a yes-and-no message, such a schizophrenic concept to cheat us from what Christ achieved for us. Mankind can no longer be identified by fallen Adam, if Christ indeed succeeded in being the last Adam. (1 Cor 15:45)

Let's summarise before we move on. Redemption is not a specific act in the life of Jesus - it can't be limited to His death or any other event, but rather it begins and is completed within the incarnation. His death, resurrection and ascension (to which we will give more attention later) are all part of, and happen within the context of the incarnation, of the God-man union in the person of Christ.

... OLD TESTAMENT PICTURES OF REDEMPTION ...

The Old testament mainly uses three words to describe redemption. There is an obvious overlap in the meaning of these words, but each of them also has a distinct emphasis.

1. Padah

The first Hebrew word we'll examine is padah.

When this word is used, the emphasis is usually on the cost of redemption and the nature of the act of redemption. Interestingly the object of redemption is always a living thing and so the substitutionary idea of a life for a life developed.

The primary use of padah is in relation to the redemption of Israel out of Egypt. (Ex 13:14, Deut 9:26; 13:5, 15:15.)

Padah is used to describe the redemption of God's people, God's property, out of an oppressive alien power and out of the judgement of God. Israel's redemption included both a deliverance from Egypt - the alien power - as well as from the angel of death which was sent by God. The redemption therefore included a sacrifice - the passover lamb.

At no time is there any hint of a ransom paid to the enemy. God did not bargain with Egypt or pay a ransom for Israel, because Israel never belonged to Egypt!

2. Kipper, kopher (redeem, ransom)

Kipper is used to describe redemption in terms of the act of wiping out sin or debt; to nullify its effect by the provision of a sacrifice. It is used both in the context of the law (Ex 21:28-30) and within the context of the priestly rituals of atoning sacrifices.

The judgement of God has been misunderstood by many. However, in order to understand redemption, we need to understand judgement. God's righteous judgement is not an attribute in contradiction to His love - God is not in conflict with Himself. His just judgement is as much part of His love as His forgiveness.

God's wrath and judgement is against anything that brings

separation, against anything that tries to reduce the pure and intimate relationship He designed, to something less. It is exactly because He loves man that He judges sin. His judgement is not against true man as such, but against anything that would reduce man to less than His original design. God will not settle for an inferior relationship.

However, man is responsible for allowing or inviting the separation; responsible for choosing an alternative and lesser way of life. As such, man took within himself that which is subject to God's righteous judgement. Man has no means by which to reverse this situation.

But God devised a way in which He could be both just and the justifier of men; a way in which He could judge sin completely and destroy its separating effect without destroying man. He provides the atoning sacrifice for man and thereby reconciles man back to Himself. He both judges and forgives in the same act. Atonement is not a way of covering the face of God so that He does not notice sin. No! It's God's way of covering and protecting man while He judges sin and destroys it.

This made the sacrificial system of Israel different from all other cults. The pagan sacrifices were meant to appease their gods. However, the Old Covenant sacrifices were commissioned by God - it was His initiative to atone for and save His people from their sins. God provides the atonement! (Deut 21:8; Ps 65:3)

3. Gaal, goel (redeem, redeemer)

The focus here is primarily on the nature of the redeemer. It has a rich and beautiful background in the family-property law, referring to redemption out of bankruptcy or bondage by a kinsman (relation) who is bound to the person in trouble both in blood and in the community of property.

When the verb gaal is used, it means to lay claim on something that has been lost or forfeited. When the noun goel is used, it describes the claimant who on the basis of a relationship of responsibility, qualifies as the redeemer. The object of redemption can either be property or a person who has sold themselves into slavery. The book of Ruth is the best example of this in the Old Testament.

... *THE REALITY OF REDEMPTION IN CHRIST* ...

These pictures give us such beautiful insight into the redemption in Christ Jesus. Jesus comes to this world as the rightful owner and as mankind's next of kin. He comes as one bound to humanity, already in relationship with humanity because of our common origin; He comes to lay claim on His own; He comes claiming our cause as His own. His relationship with humanity is demonstrated in the most fundamental way as He becomes flesh of our flesh and bone of our bone.

It's interesting to note that those who are redeemed, do not become related to the redeemer after redemption, or when they accept redemption. Redemption is only possible because the redeemer is already related to those whom he redeems! Our redemption in Christ Jesus is predicated on the fact that He is related to mankind - we have the same origin.

Mankind belongs to God. Evil never had a legitimate claim on, or ownership of man. Redemption in Christ Jesus includes both a deliverance from an alien oppressive power as well as deliverance from the just judgement of God against sin. And this redemption comes at the highest price.

When the uniquely begotten son of God becomes flesh, He takes on humanity's cause as His own. He faces the alien power not as a remote God, but He enters the arena of conflict, fully identified with man's slavery and weakness. Jesus faces temptation, in which His identity is questioned. He is given every opportunity to question God and is offered the opportunity to submit to an alternative authority (Matt 4), but He refuses. Even though He was born of a woman, part of the race under the curse of Adam's disobedience, He refuses this false identity. He remains perfectly obedient to the only rightful authority and because of His perfect obedience He condemns this lesser identity in the flesh thereby opening the way for us to once again be our true selves.

In Rom 7 Paul speaks about man's condition under the law; he speaks about this alien force or government within him that forced him to do what he did not want to do. This is slavery to sin, slavery to a way of thinking and consequently a way of acting that is far inferior to our original design. But even in this state, Paul still acknowledges that sin is not a natural attribute of man, but something separate from him, yet present within him. Despite man's best efforts, the conclusion is clear: man is powerless to free himself, to redeem himself.

This reminds me of what Jesus said about entering a strong man's house. (Matt 22:29) Sin found a home in human flesh and became a strong and enslaving presence. However, a stronger man entered the house and bound sin, spoiling his goods! Christ entered the human body and condemned sin in flesh. Sin has no independent power or influence outside of your co-operation and consent. A stronger one has come and has given the opportunity for us to reign and rule in life, even in our body of flesh. This flesh body has now become the temple, the dwelling place of the Most High God!

There are no half measures in this redemption. In order for this to be a complete redemption the separation, the lie, the false authority which man embraced in Adam, had to face the judgement of God and be destroyed. Jesus did not shun this judgement. Unlike fallen man, he did not try and justify himself or hide behind a self-righteousness. He accepted the judgement. He fully identified with man, became sin with the sinfulness of all humanity and allowed the righteous judgement of God to deal with sin in the most final way possible.

Man's justice is so often simply a way to get even. We want people to get what they deserve ... especially if someone else did something wrong! We tend to judge ourselves by our good intentions and others by their deeds. It is so important to understand that God's justice is not the selfish desire to satisfy His own offense. God's justice is restorative and healing. He judges for the purpose of bringing healing and wholeness to man. His justice, therefore, does not give us what we deserve, but what we need to be healed.

It is precisely in this judgement that the forgiveness of God is revealed. Christ offers the perfect sacrifice, the ultimate atonement, in which He, as the representative of man, bears the judgement. Allowing the judgement of God to run its full course and destroy every obstacle, every bit of the alien power that kept man in bondage, He destroys sin in the flesh, yet preserved the true man. As such, He becomes the holy, blameless and innocent man that God always had in mind. Rom 4:25 - *who was delivered up because of our offenses, and was raised because of our justification.* His resurrection is the proof of our justification. In Christ Jesus, God reconciled the world unto Himself, not holding men's trespasses against them. (2 Cor 5:19).

History records the death of one man, eternity records the death of fallen mankind : ... *because we judge thus: that if One died for all, then all died* (2 Cor 5:14) ... and the resurrection of a new humanity, a whole new creation that stands reconciled and blameless before their rightful owner.

Come, and let us return to the LORD;
For He has torn, but He will heal us;
He has stricken, but He will bind us up.
After two days He will revive us;
On the third day He will raise us up,
That we may live in His sight.
Let us know,
Let us pursue the knowledge of the LORD.
Hos 6:1-3

Our kinsman redeemer has taken our cause as His own, delivered us from the alien power of sin and faced the just judgement of God, thereby destroying the power of sin. He now reveals our true identity.

Heb 2:11 *Because both he who carried out the act of rescue and those whom he rescued and restored to innocence originate from the same source, he proudly introduces them as members of his immediate family.* (Mirror Translation)

This redemption is not only a redemption out of slavery, debt, guilt and deception, but a redemption into: Out of slavery, into the freedom of being ourselves; out of debt, into abundance - our rightful portion; out of guilt, into innocence. He rescues us out of the kingdom of darkness into the kingdom of light where the truth about God and the truth about ourselves is revealed. He succeeded in His purpose of making the Father known, and of making our own unique identity known in the bosom of the Father. *"And we know that the Son of God has come and has given us an understanding, that we may know Him who is true; and we are in Him who is true, in His Son Jesus Christ. This is the true God and eternal life."* 1 John 5:20 NKJV

CHAPTER 7
WORD PICTURES

... LOGOS, REMA & DABAR ...

The first time I heard a teaching on Logos and Rema (or Rhema), I must have been about 12 years old, but I can still remember the impression it made. The idea was basically that Logos referred to the written word or the history of God's dealing with man as recorded in the Bible, which for a 12 year old boy was all the boring, out-of-date stuff.

However, rema referred to the now, up-to-date spoken word of God! Wow - this sounded so much more relevant to my life. What a joy to discover that God still speaks! The example of the manna in the desert made so much sense - the Israelites were only given enough to eat for one day, if they collected more it would rot. The moral of the story was that we needed to hear God daily - yesterday's message was stale and unfit for consumption.

In the Christian circles I moved in this rema word soon became the focus - it was all about hearing God's guidance for today; seeking His will for today. Subtly, but surely the substance of this gospel, which is the person of Christ, was replaced by a shallow obsession to get the next prophesy, to participate in the next move of God. The eternal significance of Christ was replaced by this desperation to be current and in so doing, the essence of this gospel was replaced by something so temporary and shallow.

It's so contrary to what Paul saw in the gospel: "*We, of course, have plenty of wisdom to pass on to you ... but it's not popular wisdom, the fashionable wisdom of high-priced experts that will be out-of-date in a year or so ... It's not the latest message, but more like the oldest—what God determined as the way to bring out his best in us, long before we ever arrived on the scene.*" 1 Cor 2:6-10 MSG

I'm so glad that in this gospel, we are dealing with nothing less than the original and authentic thought and being of God Himself, which is as relevant today as it has always been.

When John starts writing his gospel, he writes about the Word (Logos) which was in the beginning - before creation and long before one word of scripture was ever written. This Word is original and authentic and what it communicates is nothing less than the person of God Himself! Obviously, this does not refer to the written word, but to the person of Christ.

So let's have a look at these words - logos and rema - again, because in them are revealed some beautiful truths about Christ. Logos and rema do not compete - they both describe the action and meaning of Christ.

It is obvious in John's writing that when he uses the Greek words *logos* and *rema*, he draws from a very definite and rich Hebrew understanding of the word dabar. If you are interested in the detailed word study then have a look at Thomas Torrance's book - Incarnation, page 58. I'll just get straight to the conclusion of the meaning of these words.

The Hebrew word dabar referred to the '*hintergroud*' or background. For instance the back-side of the tabernacle, the holy of holies was called the *debir*. Moving from the Hebrew language to Greek, John had two words he could use to convey the meaning of dabar. The word has a twofold significance. When it speaks of the inner reality or meaning of a thing, it is translated as logos. But it can also refer to a thing, an event or a piece, and this is then translated as rema. The word 'history' in Greek is *remata*. Dabar speaks about an event with a background of meaning! There is a Hebrew saying: where word and event coincide, there is truth. Can you see where this is going!

The event of Christ made known the inner reality, the mystery, the authentic thought of God. The concept of the tabernacle, the meeting place in which God and man met, was realised in the event of Christ. "*The Word became flesh and tabernacled in us. We have seen His glory, the glory of the One and Only, who came from the Father, full of grace and truth.*" The Holy of Holies, the Word that was in the bosom of the Father, has become a living event and in so doing has made known the inner reality of the Father. The meaning of God's being, coincided with the event of Christ and truth was displayed in all its glory.

Neither supernatural signs nor philosophical wisdom should ever be allowed to distract us from the wisdom of this event. (1 Cor 1: 22-25)

Paul once wrote about supernatural gifts and manifestations that are worthless and as empty as clanging cymbals - they don't even have a trace of benefit in them! It is possible to live amongst supernatural manifestations, just like the children of Israel in the desert, yet die in unbelief! The daily manna, the supernatural provision, did not do anything but sustain their desert-existence. God is interested in giving you so much more than daily manna - He wants to be the permanent sustenance within you so that you will never hunger again! Obviously, there are genuine supernatural gifts and manifestations that confirm rather than distract from the revelation of Christ.

Heb 4 says that God invited them daily to a much greater reality, a place of rest. But what 'unbelief' prevented them from entering the promised land? They believed a lie concerning themselves. In their own eyes they were like grasshoppers - they never saw their own true identity.

Recognising His voice daily is such a joy, but the best way to learn to recognise His voice is by becoming acquainted with what He has said already in Christ. Remember the sheep that were familiar with the Shepherd's voice? The incarnation, the union of God and man in the person of Christ is still the full content of what God has to say today. This is not an event that has passed away, it continues in the form of Christ in you! The incarnation continues in you!

... Now! ...

Far from diminishing the importance of the 'now' word, this greatly intensifies it. The reality of Christ in me is an ever present reality that gives substance and significance to every moment. This gives birth to the most radical attitude towards life!

Forget about trying to find His plan for your life – your life is His plan! Neither your location nor your timing matters – He has dawned His eternal day. You are His moment; you are His location! "...*worship the Father neither here at this mountain nor there ... It's who you are...*" John 4:21-23 MSG

Our hope is no longer connected to a future date but to a

person within us – all that we could ever have hoped for! Christ in you the hope of glory!

There is nothing in your future that can add anything to you! "*…the world, life, death, the present, the future—all of it is yours…*" 1 Cor 3:22 MSG. Therefore you can remove the focus and every expectation you ever had, off a future date, and instead place it on the One who is within you. The greatest gift the future holds is the unveiling of the reality within you – Christ!

Eternity entered time when God became man. The event of Christ is described as the fullness of time in Eph 1. This means that time can no longer add to the completeness of what He has already accomplished for us!

The only value that remains in the past or the future, is its ability to connect you with the present … I AM. The time-context in which God desires to encounter with you is made plain in His name: I AM! He desires for you to become conscious of this same moment – I AM. Not 'I will be'; Not 'I used to be'; Not 'I hope to be' but the overwhelming awareness that I AM. I am all He ever purposed for me to be. I have all He ever purposed for me to have.

"*Today this Scripture is fulfilled in your hearing.*" (Luke 4:21) The fulfillment of scripture has nothing to do with a calendar anymore – it has everything to do with your hearing!

Discover that the eternal One made His home in you, giving you access to eternity in this moment. Eternity has nothing to do with endless time – it has everything to do with the quality of fellowship and unity with God. (John 17:3)

"He who grasps (understands) the Son, grasps eternal life. He who does not grasp the Son, does not grasp life" (1 John 5:12)

... FROM FRAGMENTS TO FULLNESS ...

"Throughout ancient times God spoke in many fragments and glimpses of prophetic thought to our fathers.

Now, the sum total of his conversation with man has finally culminated in a son. He is the official heir of all things. He is, after all, the author of the ages. (Sonship, as represented in Jesus, is the crescendo of God's conversation with man).

We have our beginning and our present being in him. He is the force of the universe, sustaining everything that exists by his eternal utterance! Jesus is the radiant and flawless expression of the person of God. He makes the glory (intent) of God visible and exemplifies the character and every attribute of God in human form. (Gen.1:26, 27)

This powerful final utterance of God (the incarnation) is the vehicle that carries the weight of the universe. He is the central theme of everything that exists. The content of his message celebrates the fact that God took it upon himself to successfully cleanse and acquit mankind."
Heb 1:1-3 Mirror Translation

Jesus is the complete, entire and final word of God. God has nothing more to say than what He said in Christ! I have witnessed so many well-meaning believers waiting for every new word, every new wave, every new prophesy, swept to and fro by every wind of 'new revelation'. To wait for another word, another event, is to misinterpret and consequently devalue what God has said in Christ.

What we discover in Christ is not a fashionable 'now' word, but rather the original authentic thought of God! It might be fresh in our appreciation or new in our understanding, but God is not busy thinking out a new message every day – everything He wanted to say was said in absolute clarity in Christ Jesus. We need to wake up to that reality.

When the Word became flesh, it was not just a portion of the Word. Jesus is not just another fragment, another piece of God's self-revelation. No! He is the full and complete revelation of God; the crescendo of His conversation with man. In His person He communicates the word concerning the union of God and man. It's the conversation concerning eternal companionship. It's a meaningful conversation that can only take place between beings on the same level – God-kind of beings. It's the Word so large and complete that sounds and text could never adequately express it – only life, as God imagined it, is a fit medium for communicating this word.

All the stories, prophesies and religious rituals and habits served their purpose as shadows ... shadows that have become irrelevant in the light of the substance that has come in Christ. If indeed Gods spoke His final word in Christ there is no longer any room for any other religious topic outside of the revelation of Christ! Heb 12:25: "*If Jesus is the crescendo of God's final utterance, you cannot afford to politely excuse yourself from this conversation.*"

"*Take your lead from Jesus. He is your reference to a complete life. Yesterday is being confirmed today and today mirrors tomorrow. What God spoke to us in Christ is as relevant now as it was in the prophetic past and will always be in the eternal future!*" (Heb 13:8 Mirror What God began in Christ He now continues in Christ in us - it is inexhaustible.

Chapter 8
The Contradiction of the Cross

We saw earlier, in the chapter on the origin and nature of evil, that a conflict began between the possibilities God chose and created, and the possibilities He rejected and consequently did not create. These alternative possibilities were given space and opportunity when Adam chose what God rejected. The conflict between what is and what is not; the conflict between life and death; the conflict between God's authentic design and the unauthentic alternative chosen by Adam, began.

This conflict was contained, but simultaneously intensified by the introduction of the Law and the sacrificial system. Throughout this period and in the midst of a world subject to corruption and a humanity in bondage to a foreign power, God continued to speak the Word that is, the reality of what He sees, and so the contrast and pressure continued to build.

... The Climax of the Conflict ...

The death of Jesus Christ is the climax of the conflict, the ultimate confrontation. The conflict that was exposed by the law and intensified by the law, but never concluded by the law was brought to its end in Christ. The sacrificial system, which by its very repetition testified to its own failure, was finally brought to naught. For a God who '*does not require sacrifices and offerings*' the perfect sacrifice is one that forever invalidates our sacrificial systems.

The time has run out for the alternative to prove itself viable. The conflict would be brought to a conclusion in the person of Christ, as God and man finally faced each other directly. He brought the conflict to this conclusion so that we may enter His rest, His reality.

... *CONFLICT AND OBEDIENCE* ...

When the Word became flesh, He entered humanity's conflict with the express purpose of bringing it to a conclusion. The incarnation itself elevated the conflict to a new height as God's reality appeared in a world that was subjected to a lesser reality. It is the conflict of two opposing identities - the Adamic identity, characterised by sin and disobedience, and the original identity, the Son of man, characterised by His innocence and perfect obedience. Jesus' obedience in the flesh was a constant 'No!' to an alternative identity, to the state of being introduced by Adam. Simultaneously it was a 'Yes!' to God's original design and authentic concept of man. Instead of simply reflecting those around him, his family, friends and community, he remained true to the only accurate mirror of man - God.

His obedience was painfully real and culminated in death: "*He humbled Himself by becoming obedient to the point of death, even to death on a cross*" and "*He learned obedience through what He suffered*" (Phil 2:8 & Heb 5:8)

... *Conflict and Temptation* ...

Within the incarnation, there was an increase of tension and conflict which concluded in the cross. Luke 2:52 "*And Jesus increased in wisdom and in stature and in favor with God and man.*" The word 'increase' was translated from proekopten, which literally means to beat your way forward by blows. He faced temptation and resisted even to the point of sweating blood. The law of sin and death of which Paul wrote, the foreign power which forced man to do what he did not want to do, tried to gain a foothold in Christ as it had in every other man. The temptation of Christ was not limited to the 40 days in the desert. Luke tells us that "*when the devil had ended every temptation, he departed from him until an opportune time*". Shortly before His death Jesus said: "*the ruler of this world is coming, and he has nothing in Me*" John 14:30

... *The Last Adam* ...

His death on the cross was His final 'No!' to the Adamic identity; His final NO to sin; His final judgement. Separation is not a viable alternative - its only conclusion is death. The wages of sin is indeed death ... nothing less. Sin entered the world through one man, and sin was defeated and brought to naught by one man. His death was the culmination of the conflict between true man and Adamic man - man under the influence of the law of sin and death; the conflict between man as God designed him, and man as Adam imagined him. The possibility which Adam chose, the possibility which God rejected, met its final end in the last Adam.

This NO to the Adamic identity, is not just a personal choice made by the individual named Jesus. Jesus is so fully man that what He does, man does, and what happens to Him, happens to man. In Christ Jesus the whole of humanity is represented. And so Paul writes that if one died for all, then all have died! He is indeed the last Adam, the last of the Adamic race, the last man who stood condemned and guilty. Just as Adam's one act of disobedience included all men in its deathly effect, so the one act of obedience included the mass of humanity in its justifying effect.

... BUT WHY DEATH? ...

Before I even started going to school - I must have been about 4 to 5 years old - the story of Jesus' crucifixion puzzled me. My mom used to read from a children's bible about Jesus' good deeds, the way He healed people and gave hope to the condemned. Despite all these good deeds, people went ahead and killed Him! Every time I heard the story, I so desperately wanted the ending to change - there was no reason for Him to be killed! It was wrong and so utterly meaningless to murder the one who heals us.

Through many years of 'sound christian teaching' I eventually accepted that His death was not only purposeful, but that God Himself was the one who required this death!

Well, my 'puzzlement' returned and in the most amazing way brought more clarity on this event than ever before.

The cross is the greatest contradiction. It is an evil act of murder and it is our salvation. This horrific death is the ultimate goal of the accuser, satan, but simultaneously it is the event that exposes the accusation as false and so forever strips it of its power.

... THE CONTRADICTION OF THE CROSS...

This scripture summarizes the tension of this paradox: "*For the Son of Man will go just as it is written about Him, but woe to that man by whom the Son of Man is betrayed! It would have been better for that man if he had not been born.*" (Mark 14:21 HCSB)

In other words, it is part of God's plan but it is an evil act that should not happen. The scriptures simultaneously declare that he was innocent, that he was unjustly accused, that those who murdered him were guilty of the blood of all innocent victims … it was wrong in every way, yet the scriptures maintain that this was exactly what had to happen. Man's involvement and God's involvement in this event stands in complete contrast to one another.

If we become so familiar with the story that we no longer see the contradiction, then we've missed the central revelation contained in it. Like all other pagan ideas of sacrifice, much of christianity looks at this sacrifice and is mystified by its magical powers to appease God – we allow the very revelation it is supposed to bring to be swallowed up by our religious awe.

As a human act, the death of Jesus is a meaningless act of murder.
It is just another act of senseless violence.
The reason he died is because we killed him!
…just another victim of humanities brutality; another messenger, who's message made us uncomfortable, silenced forever…
And if the death of Jesus was not followed by the resurrection, then it would have remained a forgettable, meaningless event.

The murder of the innocent man Jesus Christ can never be justified – it was wrong! Even as a 5 year old, I instinctively knew that!

He was falsely accused and brutally abused by a frenzied ignorant crowd. Nowhere else was the true nature of our religious and secular institutions revealed more clearly than in this senseless violence. This is where God in all his innocence, in his most vulnerable state, faced evil in its most vivid expression – the unjustified violence of man. Evil incarnate met God incarnate.

Yet it is exactly here where evil is most real, that God intersects, turning our act of murder into our salvation. He uses the occasion of our most brutal violence to demonstrate His most extravagant love. He bore the brunt of our hostile minds, of our sinful thoughts. The event in which we bruised Him and wounded Him, is met with healing. At the very moment in which our rejection of Him is absolute, he demonstrates our absolute acceptance. It is in the very heart of this event that meaninglessness is met by significance; confusion is met by clarity; our brutality is met by God's tender mercies.

In this way the death of Jesus became humanity's death, for in the act of murdering Him, we come face to face with the emptiness of our injustice, the meaninglessness of our violence, the confusion of our wisdom, the nothingness of our imagined identity.

However, we have often ascribed both the good and the evil of the cross to God! Lets expose that myth.

... *MEN KILLED HIM, GOD RAISED HIM* ...

God obviously anticipated these events. He knew that the open display of truth, in a world bound by myth, would be a confrontation with only one possible result. The very fabric upon which our societies were build, the false accusation, the prince (principle) of this world, the father of lies, would not take to this exposure kindly. Yes, God knew and planned to make the most of this confrontation, but in no way is He the source of the violence that it exposes. In no way does He delight in the suffering and death of Jesus Christ.

Whenever the apostles spoke of the death of Christ they made it clear that He was murdered BY MEN, crucified BY MEN, killed by MEN. When they spoke about His resurrection, it is clear that God raised Him from the dead. Man is the party that kills, God is the one who reverses our evil by raising Jesus from the dead.

We continue to subject ourselves to mythical deception when we view the cross of Jesus as the punishment that satisfies God's anger; when we speak of the blood of Jesus that magically satisfies God's blood lust. These are the very fallacies the cross came to expose.

... *WHAT MAKES JESUS' BLOOD POWERFUL?* ...

God did not require the sacrifice of Jesus to enable Him to forgive. God forgave long before this event! The blood of Jesus has much greater power than the magical qualities we've assigned to it in our religious language. The blood of Jesus has unique power because it has a unique message. Before Jesus, every innocent victim's blood cried for vengeance, yet the blood of Jesus ... Jesus who identified himself with every victim ... His blood cries for forgiveness. That is its message and its power!

Theories of sacrifice that picture God as delighting in the violence, brings a schizophrenic division into the union of God, with one part of God angrily exerting his violence against man and another part lovingly taking our punishment for us. If one deconstructs this argument to its basic message it means that Jesus came to save us from the Father! The truth is, God has never been our problem! We did not need to be saved from God, but from evil.

... *VICTORY OVER EVIL* ...

Why would God then use such a paradoxical event? Revelation is both destructive and constructive; it is destructive to the deceptions it exposes and it is constructive as it lights up hidden truths.

The scriptures describe this event as God's victory over evil. Lets look at a few scriptures that describe this revelatory aspect:

1John 3:8 *The Son of God was revealed for this purpose: to destroy the devil's works.*

And we know that the Son of God has come and has given us understanding so that we may know the true One. We are in the true One—that is, in His Son Jesus Christ. He is the true God and eternal life. (1 Jn 5:20)

For so it stands written, "*I WILL EXHIBIT THE NOTHINGNESS OF THE WISDOM OF THE WISE, AND THE INTELLIGENCE OF THE INTELLIGENT I WILL BRING TO NOUGHT.*" (1Cor. 1:19 Weymouth)

The mission of Jesus is described as the destruction of the works of the accuser/accusation; as the event in which we are given understanding concerning the true God and our true selves in Him; as the public exhibition of human wisdom for the foolishness it is.

The cross both exposes evil for what it is, and reveals the goodness of God, and it does so with man as the central character. Never has evil been seen more clearly than in the brutality of mankind against an innocent victim. Never has

God been seen more clearly than in this man, Jesus Christ, willingly suffering at our hands.

... WHAT DOES THE CROSS REVEAL ABOUT EVIL? ...

Evil found its most real expression in human institutions, principalities and powers, represented by Rome, and the religious authority represented by the Sanhedrin.

The cross exposes that our very best religious dogma, the highest human philosophy about God, will sacrifice the true God for the sake of our imaginary gods. It exposes the violence of societies build upon sacrificial systems. The principalities and powers of this world, of every culture, began in false accusation escalating to murder. Human societies have violent and deceptive beginnings.

The cross exposes evil, for it reveals that it is neither the guilt of our scapegoats, nor angry gods that are the source of our suffering. We need to look for the source of evil somewhere far closer than what we are comfortable with ... we need to take seriously the biblical view that partaking of a certain knowledge is what introduced evil to this world.

In what way did He conquer evil? This was the event in which the deceiver would deceive himself; the act in which our unfounded accusations would be exposed for what they are. The story that would deconstruct all our myths into the nothingness that they are.

These false models are exposed in the very moment when our true model is revealed. We are now able to see the true God and reflect Him – a God who loves and adores; a God in whom there is no accusation.

... WHAT DOES THE CROSS REVEAL CONCERNING GOD?...

Let's first say this: if the cross is the event that God required to satisfy His need for retribution, then it has no revelatory power. That is the story that mythology has always told.

However, if the violence of the cross is not what God required, but what He endured because we required it, it reveals something totally new to mankind, something hidden from the foundation of this world. (Mt 13:35, 23:35, Lk 11:51)

Jesus, identified by John the baptist as the lamb of God, reveals that it is not our sacrifices that change the mind of God, but God's lamb that changes the mind of man. God is not the one who needs to be converted!

In the event of the cross, where God allows us to sink to our deepest alienation from Him, at the point where we are at our worst, He forgives ... it is in this moment that we are

confronted with the reality that God is not our problem –
never has been, and will never be! If when we are at our
worst, He remains forgiving, it means that we need to seek
a different party to blame for our suffering.

God has never been and never will be our problem … He
is our salvation

… ATONEMENT …

Jesus reveals the God who is with us in all the contradiction
and conflict, the God who is present even in pain, the One
who understands you better than what you understand
yourself, for He is not observing you from a distance, He
experiences everything you experience. He knows your
sitting down and your standing up, your every thought
before you think it, your every word before you say it. He
is intimately acquainted with all your ways.

Ultimately, in the person of Jesus Christ, the all-knowing,
all-powerful and all-present God, willingly lays down these
Divine privileges, subjecting Himself to our uncertainties,
our limitations and confines Himself to a human body …
in one person, in one place. He fully identifies with us. He
does all of this without ceasing to be God!

This identification culminates on the cross. This is where
an immortal God will face death; where God Himself will

feel what it is like to be godforsaken!

Jesus, taking upon Himself the mindset of fallen humanity, partakes even of our doubt and cries out: *"My God, My God, why have you forsaken me?"*

He shows the unshakable nature of his faith, not by avoiding our doubt, but by assuming our doubt and crying out on our behalf. He then proceeds to answer that question Himself, by descending into the deepest despair, the domain of evil itself, and in the midst of it all, He shows that God is still present. *"For He has not despised or detested the torment of the afflicted. He did not hide His face from him but listened when he cried to Him for help"* (Ps 22:24 HCSB)

For he hath made him to be sin for us, who knew no sin; that we might be made the righteousness of God in him. 2 Cor 5:21

In the same way in which He became sin (without personally sinning) so that we might become the righteousness of God, He fully faced and assumed our doubt, so that we might become partakers of His faith.

Jesus did not just solve our problems by waving a magic wand from afar. He entered into the middle of the conflict, stepped into the domain of contradiction, entered our hell, faced death itself and from there He conquered. Atonement is His at-one-ment with us. The early church fathers said it this way: "*What is unassumed is unhealed, but whatever He becomes, He saves*"

He demonstrates the integrity of His peace, not by avoiding our problems, but by embracing all of humanity with all of our problems and issues, without losing His peace.

He knows you, He understands you better than you understand yourself. He is fully aware of every details of your life … and He loves you. He is not uninvolved or unaware. The incarnation is the event in which God demonstrates His union with your humanity, with all its challenges and contradiction … bringing His peace to you, no matter what circumstances you find yourself in.

He demonstrates the robustness of His life, not by avoiding death, but by entering into the heart of it, and there in the midst of the greatest contradiction He bursts forth into resurrection life.

CHAPTER 9
RESURRECTION AND VICTORY

Acts 3:15 *and you killed the Author of life, whom God raised from the dead. To this we are witnesses.*
Man is responsible for the death of Jesus, God is responsible for the resurrection of Jesus. (See also Acts 2:13,24, 5:30)

If you need to understand the death and resurrection of Jesus from a legal point of view, consider the following example.

Humanity is accused in the cosmic court of the ultimate crime: you have murdered the Author of life. The charge is clear and our guilt is beyond dispute, but the story is about to take an unexpected turn...

The first witness is called.

Jesus walks into the courtroom ... very much alive.

The one we are accused of murdering takes the witness stand! This makes a verdict of "guilty of murder" very unlikely. This is why Paul says we were vindicated by the resurrection!

You see, if the death of Jesus was the legal payment for

our sin, then His death would have saved us ... and his resurrection would not even have been necessary. However Paul says in 1 Cor 15:17 ... *IF CHRIST HAS NOT BEEN RAISED, YOUR FAITH IS FUTILE AND YOU ARE STILL IN YOUR SINS.*

In other words it is not the death of Jesus that solved the sin problem, it is the resurrection.

There are two sides to justification. On one side, it is the just judgement of sin and on the other side, it is the vindication of man. "*He who was delivered over because of our transgressions, and was raised because of our justification.*" (Rom 4:25 NAS)

His death revealed our guilt, exposed the depravity of our own wisdom and religious philosophies. His resurrection reveals God's stubborn refusal to give up on man, for he knows true man - man created in His image and likeness. In the resurrection God simply reverses man's greatest evil and justifies the ungodly.

The resurrection is God's undisputed declaration that despite mankind's greatest evil, we are forgiven and declared righteous! Just as His death was the final 'No!' to the alternative man, so His resurrection is the ultimate 'Yes!' to the original man. It is the vindication and final victory of God's authentic design of man. His death brought the conflict between these options to a climax; His resurrection is the end of all conflict, the demonstration of His victory.

All contradiction between God and man, came to an end in the resurrection. This means that God's reality is now available to us. His truth which is beyond dispute or contradiction is accessible for us to live in. His Word did not return to Him void, but accomplished what He purposed. The gap between heaven and earth, His thoughts and our thoughts, His reality and our reality, has been bridged. As He is, so are we in this world!

God's love dream did not only involve removing everything that abhorred Him, but also included the restoration of the beauty and glory of all that He adores and desires. In His resurrection, mankind was restored to the blameless innocence and beauty that He loves. Our innocence is so much more than the absence of sin, it is the purity and vibrancy of being truly ourselves - our born-of-God selves. It is standing in the simplicity of our true and authentic design, fully satisfied and without any thought of an alternative existence.

The resurrection is more than just another event that follows the event of His death. Jesus said *"I am the resurrection and the life"* (John 11:25) The resurrection is Jesus Christ being Himself - living in the full reality of how God always intended for man to live. A life without any consciousness of sin, not even a consciousness of good and evil, but simply a consciousness of union with the Father. Resurrection life is a life of reigning, where the only memory of an enemy, is a memory of victory.

... *RESURRECTION AND FLESH* ...

The resurrection is a creative event in which the physical body of Jesus was restored, re-created and made fit for life once again. Resurrection is not only some abstract spiritual concept, but a life to be lived in the flesh! This is the greatest demonstration that God does not consider the human body as an obstacle to His life, but a vehicle through which to express it.

The incarnation is permanent! God has made a final choice concerning His preferred form of existence. He chose to become a man and He chose to remain a man, for in man He finds unrestrained expression. (Col 1:19; 2:9)

Rom 5:17 describes this resurrection life as one of reigning and ruling in life. Rom 6:11 describes it as unbroken or interrupted fellowship! *"Even so consider yourselves also dead to sin and your relation to it broken, but alive to God [living in unbroken fellowship with Him] in Christ Jesus."* (Rom 6:11 AMP). The implications of the resurrection are not concealed for a future day when you die! His death means that newness of life is available to us, now! The rest of Romans 6 shows how this life in the flesh is now an opportunity for God, rather than a struggle with sin.

... RESURRECTION AND CREATION ...

Redemption and specifically the resurrection is often connected with creation in New Testament thought and writing, for in it God affirms again that what He made is good and in particular, man, as His image and likeness is very good! As surely as all were included in His death, as surely all were included in His resurrection.

The new creation is God's reaffirmation of the goodness of all that He made. Evil, the alternative, the uncreated non-existent nothingness, has no claim on what God has made.

John starts his gospel by reminding us that there is indeed only one God and Creator. Everything that came from Him is original and authentic. All creation is indeed good for God created it. In the incarnation the Creator binds Himself to His creation in a way that can never be undone. The audience of redemption is nothing less than all of creation. He redeemed what He created - whether visible or invisible. Only one thing is beyond the hope of redemption and that is evil - evil is that which He did not create nor redeem.

"*The Son is the image of the invisible God, the firstborn over all creation. For in him all things were created: things in heaven and on earth, visible and invisible, whether thrones or powers or rulers or authorities; all things have been created through him and for him. He is before all things, and in him all things hold together. And he is the head of the body, the church; he is the beginning and the firstborn from among the dead, so that in everything he might have the supremacy. For God was pleased to have all his fullness dwell in him, and through him to reconcile to himself all things, whether things on earth or things in heaven, by making peace through his blood, shed on the cross.*" (Col 1:15-20 NIV)

He is the firstborn of the new creation, which is the original creation. The old has passed away, behold the new has come! We can no longer see anything or anyone from a human point of view. His resurrection has changed everything: God has reconciled everything He made to Himself in such a way that without Him nothing would be able to exist. Existence is confirmation of the presence of Christ Jesus.

... COMPLETE ...

There are many similarities we can draw between creation and redemption. One of my favourite similes is the fact that God finished creating in the first five days before He made man on the sixth. He did not create man on day one so that man could give Him a hand. He finished it all, prepared it perfectly and only then did He create man. Man's only contribution would be appreciation!

Redemption follows the same strategy. God completes it from beginning to end. He completes it from both God and man's side in the one person of Christ Jesus. Our only possible contribution is appreciation. "*declare His righteousness to a people yet to be born--that He has done it [that it is finished]!*" Ps 22:31 AMP

... *The Dawn of an Eternal Day* ...

Each of the days of creation has both a morning and an evening - a beginning and an end. However, the seventh day, the day of God's rest, has no end. God entered His rest on the seventh day because He was satisfied with what He had made. It's similar to an artist reaching the point where he lays down his brushes, stand back and simply appreciates the completed work of art.

The book of Hebrews shows how throughout history, God has invited man to this place of rest. This day represents God's reality, God's place, God's time and God's occupation. He rests in the full knowledge and satisfaction that what He made is good, that evil is temporal and has been dealt a fatal blow in Christ Jesus. He rests in the full assurance that the goodness He sees in mankind is reality and will triumph.

The resurrection is a fusion between eternity and time, between God's time and our time. Remember, Jesus said: *"I am the resurrection and the life"*. As such it is not just another event that fades with history, but it remains the ever present event in the person of Christ Jesus in which the God-man union triumphed over all contradiction and made this union a permanent reality.

The invitation into this rest, is an invitation to cease from all our efforts; to lay down our brushes with which we have tried to improve God's work of art. We enter His rest when we allow His persuasion to become ours; when we see His reality and rest in the full assurance of it. There is nothing wrong with you, because there is nothing wrong with your redemption! The resurrection is evidence of your union with God and the proof that God's reality is accessible right now, right here.

Chapter 10
Ascension and New Reality

... Glorification ...

When Jesus washed His disciples feet, He humbled Himself in this act of servanthood without losing His dignity or value. (John 13) When you are secure in the knowledge of your identity, then humbling yourself in servanthood becomes much easier, for far from reducing your identity, such deeds confirm the surety and immutability of your true identity.

Philippians 2 describes the incarnation as an act in which God humbled Himself and took the form of a servant. God Himself, became a servant to mankind! Yet, He was not reduced in person or dignity. He became man without ceasing to be God in any way.

In this sense the ascension is the inverse of the incarnation. The ascension is the glorification of Christ and of man in Christ. It is the act in which God honours Christ and in so doing restores man to the place and position of glory that He intended for us from the beginning. For just as surely as mankind was included in the death and resurrection of Christ, so we were included in His ascension.

The ascension is the act in which man is elevated again to the place of union with God. Just as God became man without ceasing to be God, so man has been united with God without ceasing to be man. Union with God does not consume man, but rather it releases man to be truly man. We remain distinctly human in union with God.

The Word that was in the beginning, even before space and time, entered our reality but remained the God beyond the limits of space and time. In the ascension we are transported to this eternal realm beyond the limits of space and time, but we also remain in this world in order to redeem time and give God space in this earthly realm.

... WHERE? ...

"Pursue with diligence the consequence of your co-inclusion in Christ. Relocate yourself mentally! His resurrection co-raised you to the same position of authority, seated in the strength of God's right hand. Becoming affectionately acquainted with Throne Room thoughts will keep you from being distracted again by the earthly (soul-ruled) realm. Your union with His death broke the association with that world; the secret of your life now is the fact that you are wrapped up with Christ in God. Every time Christ is revealed as our life, we are being co-revealed in the same glory (likeness and image of God) being united together with Him." (Col 3:1-4

The right-hand of God, a place of authority far above this earthly realm, is now our home-ground! This is the new reality we have to become acquainted with.

This place cannot be accurately described in terms of space and time, for it is the eternal realm beyond the limits of space and time. Eph 4:10 says that he descended and ascended so that He might fill all things. "*He Who descended is the same as He Who also has ascended high above all the heavens, that He might fill all things*". Created time and space has been invaded by the Creator Himself - He fills both creation and the realm beyond creation.

This eternal realm is not far from each one of us, for the limits of space and time are all around us. In Him we live and move and have our being.

Where is the throne room?
Where is this heavenly place?
Wherever Christ is!

For Christ is the place and the moment where God and man encounter each other face to face, without division, separation or confusion.

"We have our beginning and our present being in him. He is the force of the universe, sustaining everything that exists by his eternal utterance! Jesus is the radiant and flawless expression of the person of God. He makes the glory (intent) of God visible and exemplifies the character and every attribute of God in human form. (Gen.1:26, 27) This powerful final utterance of God (the incarnation) is the vehicle that carries the weight of the universe. He is the central theme of everything that exists. The content of his message celebrates the fact that God took it upon himself to successfully cleanse and acquit mankind. Jesus is now his right hand of power, seated in the boundless measure of his majesty. He occupies the highest seat of authority, in which our innocence is represented." (Hebrews 1:3 Mirror Translation)

The highest seat of authority, represents our innocence. There is nothing in God's reference to man that reminds Him of sin, for He has completely and finally dealt with it in Christ. We are now defined by Christ! In Him all things find their meaning. The summary and conclusion of man's identity and worth is found in Him.

He is seated and at rest within this reality. We are included in Him and seated with Him - we no longer have to live within the guilt and contradiction that entered the world through Adam, for we have an origin that began before

Adam and was restored in Christ. He found us in Christ before we were lost in Adam (Eph 1:4)

When the true identity of Christ is revealed, the truth about you is simultaneously revealed. "*Whenever Christ is revealed, you are revealed with Him*" (Col 3:4). We cannot separate the proclamation of Christ from the revelation of man's place within Him. That's why Paul summarises the mystery of the gospel as "*Christ in you*" and continues to say that the purpose of his instruction is to reveal man's perfection in Christ. (Col 1:26-29)

What what do we mean by 'Christ in me'? Some have asked me to clarify what I believe concerning Christ in all men, so here is a clarification:

If by 'in' we mean a living relationship, a union between Christ and a person whereby Christ can express Himself through that person .... then NO I don't believe Christ is in everyone in this context. Darkness cannot fellowship with light.

However if by 'in' we mean that Christ is the One who gives life and breath to everyone (He Himself gives to all people life and breath and all things Acts 17:25) then yes in that context I believe He is present everywhere. If by 'in' we mean that nothing can exist without Him then YES I believe He sustains everything ... the whole universe!

CHAPTER 11
CONFRONTED

In Christ Jesus, mankind is confronted with the reality of our salvation. The message of Christ in nothing less than the unveiling of God's reality - the truth as He sees it. What Christ accomplished is not potentially real or theoretically real or only legally valid, it is simply real!

He is the ultimate representation of the reality of God and the ultimate representation of the reality of man. What He accomplished is nothing less than the reconciliation of God and man. You were in Christ, in His death, in His resurrection and in His Ascension. In Christ you are confronted with the reality of your salvation.

When the Word became flesh, when God became a man, When the Creator became part of creation, He bound Himself inseparably to us. Our existence was changed by this act! We can no longer think of ourselves apart from this event, neither can we think of God apart from His initiative in becoming one with man.

His death was our death. Our guilt and sin met their final end, their final judgement when we died together with Christ. The relationship between man and sin was severed in His death and our slate was wiped clean. Every accusation that stood against us and the debt we owed was justly paid in full. The past, with all its guilt and imperfections, was consumed in this death!

We were raised together with Christ. We were restored to the men and women He had in mind since the beginning - the pure and blameless companions He imagined. We are free to be our true selves, without conflict or contradiction! In His resurrection we were restored and translated into God's reality - the kingdom of light. Time itself has been redeemed as God and man meet face to face in the resurrected Jesus Christ. He is eternally present - the new reality of my existence.

Not only were we united with God in his death and resurrection, but we were raised with Him into heavenly places. The ascension is the glorification of man to the place and position that He prepared for us - permanent union with Him.

All of this is of God, He accomplished it without our help and without our permission! It is truth whether we acknowledge it or not. As Paul said: "*We can do nothing against the truth, only for it*" (2 Cor 13:8)

... *RECONCILED* ...

One morning I woke up early as the Lord started speaking to me about 'versoening'. That is the Afrikaans word for 'reconciliation'. It implies to kiss-and-make-up. Reconciliation is used in a very intimate way in the scriptures. In a number of languages, including Afrikaans, the base word in reconcile, means to kiss.

There is a Divine kiss within reconciliation. Reconciled is the state you are in, because God kissed you! 2 Corinthians 5:19 says that God was in Christ reconciling the world to Himself. In Christ, becoming flesh, becoming man, God embraced your humanity ... He kissed your being!

Jesus Christ is fully God and fully man. In his person, there is no separation or distance between God and man. In His person God and man are one - reconciled. This is a kiss so intimate and so constant that we can no longer distinguish between God and man.

Christ's resurrection proved that this unity, this God-man union, God's kiss, was not just a temporary event. God became man in Jesus Christ, and Christ is still a man. This kiss continues!

So what is our message to mankind? Kiss back! Do not just stand there surprised and open-mouthed - kiss back! You are reconciled - God kissed.

Our life of intimacy with God is God's call to the people around us. Reconciliation is a completed fact, but it is also a continual act. Jesus represents God's continual embrace of mankind. Jesus Christ is God's constant kissing of man - kiss back!

... FAITH AND DECISION ...

So does it matter what we believe? Absolutely! Faith releases the benefit of the truth. (Heb 4:2). It is possible to continue living in ignorance and miss out on the enjoyment of what God has done for us. It is possible to continue living by our own strength and effort, ignoring the place of rest He prepared. This is why He still renews the promise daily saying: "*Today if you hear my voice, do not harden your hearts.*"

The more important question is how this faith is awakened and how man should be brought to this place of decision.

Eph 1:13 calls this message the "*word of truth, the gospel of your salvation*". This gospel is first and foremost a declaration of the truth as God knows it. It is the declaration of His persuasion. In it you are confronted with the reality of your salvation in Christ Jesus.

Rom 1:17 shows that in the gospel "*the righteousness of God is revealed from faith to faith*". It is from God's faith to our faith. Listen to how the Mirror translation says it: "*The secret of the Gospel is this: God did it right in Christ; the righteousness of God means that what happened in Christ, happened to us. His faith ignites ours. (From faith to faith) He is convinced about mankind and now persuades us to believe what He knows to be true about us. The prophets wrote in advance about this life of righteousness which would be based on faith and not on personal performance.*"

His faith ignites our faith! This is why Paul could say: "*The life I now live in the body, I live by the faith of the Son of God*" (Gal 2:20) Faith is not something we generate ourselves. The faith of God is contained within the declaration of the gospel - we can receive it or reject it, but we can never invalidate it or replace it with our own persuasions.

When man is presented with the reality of what God has done for and with man in Christ Jesus, it does not remove the need for faith, but greatly intensifies it. When we see the reality of God's opinion of us and how that contrasts with the reality of our experience, it creates a confrontation: do we want to live in God's reality or continue in the chaos and deception of our own opinions.

We also know that when anyone hears the word, he sees

the face of his birth. (James 1:23) Once we've seen the truth about ourselves, we cannot reject it without rejecting our own existence.

It has to be emphasised that even this decision is not a mechanical formula that can be enforced on a person. This decision is based on the fact that God has made a decision for us. He chose us and demonstrated His choice in Christ beyond doubt. His decision is to be one with you, to be reconciled to you, to make you His companion.

It was His choice to destroy our debt and guilt. It was His decision to unite us in His death and to present us blameless and innocent in His resurrection. It was His determined will to raise us up together with Him and seat us together with Him in heavenly places. How can we do anything but make a decision for Him, when we realise His decision for us!

God's election was demonstrated in the decisive action He took in Christ Jesus. His decision was to give Himself to us, to lavish His love upon humanity. In becoming man, He made known that His will and purpose is to be united with man. It is on the basis of this decision that we are enabled to make a decision for Him.

What does it mean to introduce someone to Christ? We would never have had the motivation or desire to travel, minister or share this gospel, if all we had to offer was another opinion or some emotional religious experience. Seeing people come into a living relationship with Christ through the declaration of this gospel, is the greatest privilege there is. Talking about God has little appeal for us ... but allowing God Himself to make His appeal through us is an experience beyond comparison.

So here are a few aspects that I am aware of, and I believe will be helpful to you, when introducing people to Christ:

1. God of initiative.

I'm so glad we are not dealing with a distant, angry God - One who suspiciously looks at your every thought and action to see if you are worthy of meeting with Him. No! Our God - God as revealed by Jesus Christ - took the initiative to meet with us. And His initiative was not limited to taking the first step. He went all the way in reconciling us to Himself. That means that everything that stood between man and God, every offense, every sin, He dealt with.

So introducing someone to Christ is in the first place not focused on what this person needs to do, say, pray or feel, but instead it is based on what God has done!

2. The God who is near.

There is nothing more attractive than an awareness of the personal presence of God. What confidence we can have when speaking to people, knowing that the One we speak of, is sustaining their very existence! He upholds them even while they are ignorant of Him. Every cell and atom in their body exists through Him and for Him. (1Cor 8:6, Col 1:16,17, Heb 1:3)

No wonder Paul speaks to unbelieving heathens in Acts 17 and even before they are able to respond or accept his message, Paul says: '*He is not far from each one of us ... In Him we live and move and have our being ... for you are indeed His offspring*'!!

"*Let all men know your gentleness and thereby recognise and become aware of the nearness of the Lord.*" Phil 4:5

In Jesus Christ, God demonstrated the union between Himself and man as He always intended it to be. In this union there is no distance of any kind between man and God. We bring an awareness of the nearness, the closeness of God through the preaching of the gospel. Such an awareness, is faith. Faith is being aware of what God is aware of.

3. Spirit-encounter.

When we introduce Christ to a person, it is in the first instance not a physical, emotional or intellectual introduction, but a spirit-encounter with spirit-reality. Yes, this encounter will affect your emotions, your intellect and your physical existence, but its source is spiritual.

Remember, God was before time and space came into existence. As we saw previously, He sustains all of creation, but we should never allow our concept of Him to be reduced to someone that can be explained or grasped in physical terms. In other words, He does fill all of creation, but He is not contained or limited by creation.

I say this because we have often allowed our understanding of 'introducing Christ' to be reduced to a physical description. God's being and the spirit realm in which He operates is a reality of infinitely greater substance than the physical. That is why some of Jesus' sayings completely challenge our understanding of time and space. For instance, He said: "*Before Abraham was, I AM*" In our linear understanding of time, this statement would be grammatically incorrect. On another occasion He said: "*In that day you will know that I am in My Father, and you in Me, and I in you.*" In our three-dimensional understanding of space, this saying does not make sense. Three entities occupying the same space simultaneously ... being both the container and the contents ... does not make sense ... in the physical.

When we declare this gospel, we can have confidence that something much wiser than human logic, and something more mysterious than supernatural signs is happening in the hearers. We have all the reason in the world to expect God to reveal Himself! Expect Spirit-encounter beyond the five physical senses; expect God to reveal through His spirit what "*eye has not seen and ear has not heard and has not entered into the heart of man*" (1 Cor 2:9)

What does this Spirit encounter reveal? "*Now we have received the ... Spirit Who is from God, that we might realise and comprehend and appreciate the gifts and blessing so freely and lavishly bestowed on us by God.*" (1 Cor 2:12)

Paul once recounted what Jesus commissioned him to do as follows: "*I now send you, to open their eyes, in order to turn them from darkness to light, and from the power of Satan to God, that they may receive forgiveness of sins and an inheritance among those who are sanctified by faith in Me.*" (Acts 26:18)

What does it mean for a person to accept Christ other than to 'open their eyes'; to turn from darkness to light! And in opening their eyes they receive and realise what has been freely given to them.

4. Meet yourself!

In meeting Christ Jesus, we meet the One who designed us, planned us, chose us and intimately knows us. We might have much to learn about Him, but He knows everything about us … and much of what can be learnt about Him will be found in what He knows about us. Christ always reveals Himself "as in a mirror", not as a separate entity. (2 Cor 3:18) He reveals Himself as the secret of your true life. (Col 3:3,4) So when you meet Christ, you meet yourself for the very first time! You meet the Author and Perfecter of your design.

What this means in practical terms is that when I speak to someone about Christ, there is no conflict between speaking about who Christ is and speaking about who He made them to be. James says that whenever this word is heard, it is like a man seeing the face of his birth as in a mirror! (James 1:23)

This encounter is described so beautifully in Ps 17:15: "*As for me, I will continue beholding Your face in righteousness; I shall be fully satisfied, when I awake in Your likeness*".

To recognise the Lordship of Jesus Christ cannot be separated from recognising His image and likeness within you. You belong to Him because He made you … and redeemed you! Awake to His reality; awake to His likeness in you!

You are part of God's gift … to you! Unwrap yourself, discover yourself, accept yourself and be thankful for such a thoughtful gift.

So what happens when a person receives Christ?
Receiving Christ is based on the truth that He already 'received', embraced and reconciled you! The scriptures reveal that grace and salvation were given to us before time began! (2 Tim 1:9). You were included in the life, death and resurrection of Christ - again, all of this happened before your birth. So in a sense, nothing changed - we simply wake up to God's reality.

Then again, everything changes for our eyes are opened for the first time when we meet Christ. The illusions and oppression of darkness loose their hold. God's reality has opportunity to find expression in your life! You start to know yourself as you have always been known. As a seed that germinates and produces after its own kind, the DNA of God is released to produces the God-kind of life He always knew was yours.

The gifts He so lavishly gave can now be adored, enjoyed

and used for the first time. Eternal truth starts displacing temporal illusions. Life, original life, breaks through the hardened soil of self imposed ideas and opinions. This life is spontaneous, fresh, new, yet it is original, the life God designed and preserved for you even before your conception.

... ROAD TO EMMAUS (LUKE 24) ...

A few days after the cruxifiction of Jesus, two disciples were walking to a town called Emmaus. The events of the past few days were fresh in their minds and the content of their conversation. However, the meaning of these events had eluded them – truth is rarely found on the surface, on the mere appearance of things.

A third traveller joined them – Jesus Himself – but they did not recognise Him. Jesus did not immediately reveal Himself or offer His opinion on the subject. He was interested in conversation, not one-sided instruction.

Verse 17: *And He said to them, What is this discussion that you are exchanging between yourselves as you walk along? And they stood still, looking sad and downcast.*

Cleopas answered and gave a factually accurate description of the events. But we can see that their perspective of these events left them with the wrong conclusions: they were sad and downcast.

Jesus sees the same events, but from a different perspective. Faith lifts us to a place where we can see from God's point of view.

Verse 25-27 *"And [Jesus] said to them, O foolish ones and slow of heart to believe everything that the prophets have spoken! Was it not necessary and essentially fitting that the Christ should suffer all these things before entering into His glory? Then beginning with Moses and all the Prophets, He went on explaining and interpreting to them in all the Scriptures the things concerning and referring to Himself."*

It is significant that at this point, Jesus once again refrains from simply revealing Himself. Instead He considers it important for these disciples to understand the scriptures … thoroughly! The journey was about 7 miles (12 km) so they had time for a comprehensive discussion. Perception, understanding and insight is obviously part of God's strategy for us to encounter Him – it is part and parcel of the experience of Christ. Had He simply revealed Himself, without engaging in conversation, without expounding the scriptures and without presenting to them a completely new point of view, their experience of Christ might well have been more shallow, not engaging their whole being.

Verse 28-31: *"Then they drew near to the village where they were going, and He indicated that He would have gone farther."*

What happened here is so important to understand. Jesus does not try and 'close the deal'. He does not try and force a decision. After this whole period of ministry and teaching, He does not end it with an invitation to accept or reject what He said. He simply indicates that He would be going further!

Jesus knew that He took them as far as He could in their understanding of the truth. The point of decision was not a place into which He would push them.

"But they constrained Him, saying, "Abide with us, for it is toward evening, and the day is far spent." And He went in to stay with them. Now it came to pass, as He sat at the table with them, that He took bread, blessed and broke it, and gave it to them. Then their eyes were opened and they knew Him; and He vanished from their sight." (verse 29-31)

Let's present the gospel in such a way, that the hearers constrain us to stay. Let's not use the latest sales techniques to artificially draw out a response. The Word of truth contains the faith of God. It has everything in it to awaken the appropriate response.

Presenting the gospel in this way, without artificially eliciting a response, does not take away the urgency of responding, it increases the urgency! When the truth is revealed without any conditions attached, it means that the choice is even clearer: embrace the truth or live in deception and confusion. As mentioned before, once we've seen the truth about ourselves, we cannot reject it without rejecting our own existence.

CHAPTER 12
THE INCARNATION
CONTINUES

"I continually thank my God for you because of the grace of God which is given you in Christ Jesus, that you are enriched by Him in every possible way, in all the fullness of what can be known and understood and being able to express it fully. Just as the evidence of Christ was confirmed within you - you have within yourselves the proof that He is! You don't lack anything - you are fully qualified. You have every reason to expect the Lord Jesus Christ to be made visible through you. Who also confirms your blamelessness to the uttermost degree in the day of our Lord Jesus Christ."
(1 Cor 1:4-8 AR Translation)

Verse 5: ... *in all utterance (logos) and all knowledge* (gnosis).

The same logos that John wrote of - the logos that was in the beginning with God, and was God, the logos that became flesh in the person of Christ Jesus - this is the same logos with which we have been enriched. He has enriched us with all of Himself! Not just a portion or a fragment, but everything He is has been deposited in you. The same logos that became flesh in Christ, now becomes flesh in you! Col 2:3 speaks about all the treasures of wisdom and knowledge that are hidden in Him. If you have Him - you have all the treasures of wisdom and knowledge!

This enrichment, this immeasurable deposit is not meant to remain quiet, unseen and undisturbed deep within you. We have every reason to expect Christ to express himself through us - an expression as full and accurate as the logos that was deposited in us. He anticipates that His DNA, from which you were born, would produce His God-kind of life in and through you. God sees no reason to expect any lesser manifestation of His life in you than in Jesus. You don't lack anything - you are fully qualified. You have every reason to expect the Lord Jesus Christ to be made visible through you.

The opening statement of the book of Acts is so enlightening. Luke writes "*about all that Jesus began to do and teach*". Jesus began something that now continues in us! In Acts 3 we read the story of Peter and John meeting a lame man on their way to the temple. This happened shortly after the ascension of Christ, so one could imagine Peter saying: "*I'm sorry, you've just missed Him. If only Jesus was still with us, we might have been able to offer you something*". Neither does Peter give the very spiritual advice that we have so often heard: "*Don't look at us - look at Jesus*"! No! Peter says: "*Look at us*" and then proceeds to heal this man!

Peter and John understood that what Jesus began, did not end at His ascension. They understood that the same Logos, the same person that was manifested in Christ Jesus, was now at home in them. They understood that the incarnation continues; that God has united Himself with man, that His thoughts and person continues to find expression in those who accept the union He brought about in Christ.

... DISCOVER GREAT TREASURE ...

Paul spoke about treasure in earthen vessels. (2 Cor 4:7) In another letter He wrote about the "the riches of His glorious inheritance in the saints" (Eph 1:18)

Jesus spoke about this same treasure when He said: "*the kingdom of heaven is like treasure hidden in a field, which a man found and hid; and for joy over it he goes and sells all that he has and buys that field*". (Matthew 13:44)

God has invested everything He has, everything He is, in mankind. His treasure, His inheritance is located nowhere else but in mankind. The image and likeness of our Creator is what gives every man value. Proverbs speaks about the wisdom of God that was in the beginning. The same wisdom that John wrote about when he said the Word became flesh in the person of Christ. This is what proverbs says about this Wisdom: "*Then I was beside Him as a master craftsman; And I was daily His delight, Rejoicing always before Him, Rejoicing in His inhabited world, And my delight was in the sons of men."* (Pr 8:30,31)

God's joy and delight has always been in the children of men! If God's inheritance is in man, if He saw a treasure within humanity for which He paid the highest price, then we can find no greater value, no greater treasure than where He finds it. The greatest joy, delight and treasure, lies hidden in the next person you see!

It is this knowledge that inspired Paul to write that when it pleased God to reveal His Son in him, his immediate urgency was to proclaim Him (Christ) in the nations. *"This mystery has been kept in the dark for a long time, but now it's out in the open. God wanted everyone, not just Jews, to know this rich and glorious secret inside and out, regardless of their background, regardless of their religious standing. The mystery in a nutshell is just this: Christ is in you, so therefore you can look forward to sharing in God's glory. It's that simple."* (Col 1:26,27 MSG, Gal 1:16)

Recognising Christ, God's original design and blueprint of mankind, God's image and likeness in flesh form, is what drove Paul beyond the point of duty, to instruct every man about their perfection in Christ Jesus.

I love the way the Mirror Translation says this:

"This mystery was concealed for ages and generations but is now fully realised in our restored innocence before Him. (God knows the mineral wealth that He deposited in the earth on man's behalf) in the same way He now eagerly anticipates the unveiling of the riches of the ultimate treasure in all the nations; which is Christ in you! The revelation of His indwelling fulfills His dream for you. This is the essence and focus of our message; we awaken every man's mind instructing every individual, bringing them into full enlightenment in order that we may exhibit the whole of mankind as perfect (without shortcoming and fully efficient) in Christ. To accomplish this, I am laboring beyond the point of exhaustion striving with intense resolve with all the energy that He mightily inspires within me." (Col 1:26-29)

I think Paul's whole motivation is summed up in Eph 3:9: *"to make all men see what is the fellowship of the mystery, which from the beginning of the ages has been hidden in God who created all things through Jesus Christ"*. What he saw inspired him to make all men see, to go to any extent to help others see Christ in themselves, and themselves in Christ.

... *ETERNAL INHERITANCE* ...

Our inheritance is so much more than a few perks we get for serving God! Our inheritance is exactly the same as God's inheritance: the treasure within man. I want to encourage you to discover this treasure in the people around you and in people far away. Don't limit your life to your job description; don't limit your life to some religious concept of special gifts and callings.

Part of the joy of finding great treasure is the pursuit, the journey, the adventure of searching for it beyond your familiar comfort zone. We have been enriched in so many ways by the friends we've discovered, both near and far. Some were local, but this awareness of value took us beyond our local community. Throughout the world Christ is waiting to be discovered in people.

"Ask of Me, and I will give You the nations as Your inheritance, and the uttermost parts of the earth as Your possession." (Ps 2:8). God has hidden treasure for each of us, in all the nations. He sees the impact of your life, uncontrollably expanding beyond your locality. Nothing but the uttermost parts of the earth is your inheritance! On one occasion Mother Teresa was asked why she chose to serve the poorest of the poor and part of her reply was: *"to discover Christ in the most distressing disguise!"*

What I also discovered is that there will never be a convenient time or situation for one to start going into all the nations. Your circumstances will never provide the inspiration to go into all the world – only what you see, the treasure in earthen vessels, will inspire you to go. While in normal full-time employment, I made a decision not to wait for a convenient time to start going into all the world, but to simply take every opportunity. In that year we visited a number of countries and what a joy it has been!

David wrote the most inspired Psalms while fleeing for his life before a king who was set on killing him. Paul wrote the most joyful letter while in prison awaiting the sentence of death.

See what God sees and then do what He does. God loves to the uttermost and will go anywhere to demonstrate his love. You don't need a special invitation from the Lord to take the good news to the nations. He made known his will long ago when He said "*All authority in heaven and earth has been given to me. Therefore go into all the world and make disciples of all nations ... and behold I am with you always*" (Matthew 28

The conclusion of "*All authority in heaven and earth has been given to me*" is "*Therefore go*". Make use of what is yours; give what you have been given. He is with us, in us, for us and eager to manifest Himself - put yourself in positions where His supernatural life and authority is needed!

MORE RESOURCES AVAILABLE AT:

HTTP://HEARHIM.NET

FOR ONLINE CONVERSATIONS AND STUDY MATERIAL SEE:

HTTP://GINOMAI.ORG/

Andre & Mary-Anne Rabe